Dedication

This book is dedicated to those missionaries and their families, God's storm troopers, who have given all to bring Christ's good news to the far-flung frontiers of the earth.

This book is also dedicated to my wife, Glenda, whose walk with Christ, prayers, support, and love have been my joy and strength.

This book is also dedicated to our children, Julianne and Jennifer, their husbands, and our grandchildren—all of whom have brought great joy into our lives.

Most of all, this book is dedicated to the Lord Jesus Christ, who came to give life—eternally and abundantly. He alone is Savior and Lord.

What others are saying about this book . . .

"All missionaries experience stress, and missionary families especially are stressed. It is part of our job description. Dr. Jere Phillips has written a book that will help and encourage stressed missionaries. Reading it will aid missionaries already on the field, and those in training will benefit from the book also. Missions administrators and leaders should read this book so they can help hurting missionaries. As one who served overseas for more than twenty years, I can attest to the reality of missionary stress, and I'm glad to have a book like this to recommend to hurting missionaries. Truly, this book should be required reading for all those who serve in a missions setting."

—Dr. John Mark Terry, long-time field missionary, seminary professor, and author, including *Missiology: An Introduction* and *Developing a Strategy for Missions*

"Dr. Jere Phillips has given missionaries—current, future, and former—a practical tool for dealing with stress. Missionaries know they can come to Jesus as they are 'weary and heavy laden' in order to find rest. Often, practically speaking, that rest is hard to find. Rest, through Christ, is possible however. Dr. Phillips gives simple but thorough ideas as to how one can deal with some common stressors on the field. With his Christ-centric approach, missionaries can understand their stress but also learn how they can move forward and thrive in both their ministries and personal lives."

—Dr. Jeff Brawner, former missionary and chair of the Missions Department of Mid-America Baptist Theological Seminary

"As a missionary serving in an area where my name or location cannot be revealed, . . . this is a very helpful book. It is filled with useful information that anyone serving on the field can use, whether serving in the US or around the world. I recommend this book to all who leave their home cultures to serve in new cultures. This book might just save a marriage, a career, or a person's calling."

—Name withheld due to security concerns

THE MISSIONARY FAMILY:

Managing Stress Effectively

Jere L. Phillips, PhD

innovo
PUBLISHING

Published by
Innovo Publishing, LLC
www.innovopublishing.com
1-888-546-2111

innovo
PUBLISHING

Providing Full-Service Publishing Services for
Christian Authors, Artists & Organizations: Hardbacks, Paperbacks,
eBooks, Audiobooks, Music & Film

THE MISSIONARY FAMILY:
Managing Stress Effectively
Copyright © 2013 Innovo Publishing

Unless otherwise indicated, Scripture is taken from the King James Version. (Note: Author has
changed some wording, such as "thee" and "ye" to "you," for ease of reading.)

Library of Congress Control Number: 2013922293
ISBN 13: 978-1-61314-180-9

Cover Design & Interior Layout: Innovo Publishing, LLC

Printed in the United States of America
U.S. Printing History

First Edition: December 2013

About the Author

The author has over forty years of experience in ministry, including extensive missions experience in the United States and overseas. While in college, he served as a church-planting summer missionary in Oregon. After serving as pastor and staff minister in Tennessee, Louisiana, and Florida, he became the director of the Missions Department of the Tennessee Baptist Convention and then served as executive director of the West Virginia Convention of Southern Baptists. A professor at Mid-America Baptist Theological Seminary since 2001, he also has served in numerous interim pastorates.

Dr. Phillips has traveled to twenty-six countries on six continents, including multiple missions to several countries. He has worked with missionaries, regional mission leaders, and indigenous pastors. Phillips has provided training for national and regional leaders for several Baptist Unions in sixteen trips to countries of the former Soviet Union. He has been recognized by the Russian Union of Evangelical Christians—Baptists for service to its denominational leaders and pastors across the nation.

Phillips earned his Master of Divinity and Doctor of Philosophy degrees from New Orleans Baptist Theological Seminary, including a major in preaching and minor in psychology and counseling. His doctoral study included Advanced Clinical Pastoral Education at Central Louisiana Psychiatric Hospital.

The Phillipses have two married daughters and seven grandchildren. Their oldest daughter, Julianne, and her family live in Collierville, Tennessee, where they are active leaders at Germantown Baptist Church. Their youngest daughter, Jennifer, and her family serve as missionaries in Brisbane, Australia.

Table of Contents

Foreword

Jerry Rankin, President Emeritus
International Mission Board, SBC

When my family and I left for the mission field in Indonesia more than forty years ago, we envisioned an exciting adventure of taking the gospel to the largest populated Muslim nation in the world. We were absolutely confident of our call and expected to see the miraculous hand of God at work in response to our commitment and obedience. Needless to say, our initial experience was filled with disillusionment, as we were blindsided by the stress of cross-cultural challenges and adjustments.

Unfortunately, our experience was not unique in spite of the efforts of mission-sending agencies to prepare candidates for the realities of the missionary experience. Seeking to cope with the challenge of language learning and establish a presence in a foreign setting is a formidable task. Hampered by limited communication skills, inability to understand contradictory worldviews, and failure to perceive societal mores create confusion and self-doubts. Isolated from family, friends, and a supportive church fellowship back home, the missionary family is overwhelmed with debilitating stress.

Add to the adjustment challenges the lack of sanitation, chaotic traffic, congested cities, and intolerable heat, and the mission field becomes a matter of survival rather than fulfilling ministry. One finds himself in a dysfunctional bureaucracy that demands time-consuming processes for foreign registration, visa renewal, and efforts to ensure elusive security for the family. It should be a surprise that attrition in missionary service is no higher than it is. No one venturing into cross-cultural ministry is exempt from stress; it goes with the territory, is common to all, and the most blatant symptom is the toll it takes on the family.

Sometimes it takes an outsider to best discern realities that are obscured by subjective experiences. Dr. Jere Phillips has served for forty-three years in church ministry, denominational leadership, and theological education. These roles have been a springboard for his passion for the Great Commission and extensive involvement in dozens of short-term mission opportunities all over the world. He has trained national workers, led missionary conferences, and worked alongside them in a plethora of projects and evangelistic outreach. He has stayed with missionary families and has become a trusted confidante. His reading and scholarly study has equipped him with insight into both the problem and solution to stress on the mission field.

This little volume, *The Missionary Family: Managing Stress Effectively*, is a valuable resource in preparation of the missionary candidate as well as a source of helpful insights to those already on the field. It will help families and churches at home to be understanding and sympathetic to the problems of personnel overseas and, rather than being quick to judge, help them to know how to provide ministry and encouragement.

Phillips explores the causes of stress to highlight that it is not always the foreignness of the mission field and demanding lifestyle that are the cause. One's temperament, lack of self-confidence, spiritual immaturity, and passion of the call, among other factors, contribute to the problem. It is especially helpful to note how stress is manifested and its impact on the children and family. Conflict with colleagues, health problems, and an erosion of faith are caused by stress and contribute to ineffectiveness as well as burnout and resignation.

Incidentally, the issues dealt with in this book are not unique to overseas workers but are common to those in ministry at home. Readers identifying with the symptoms of stress will be tempted to jump to the final section, a thorough discussion of ways to manage it, noting it is not a matter of avoiding stress but how to deal with it. It is not surprising that Phillips highlights this as a spiritual issue with spiritual and biblical solutions. But there are also mental, emotional, physical, and social aspects in gaining victory over stress.

The missionary is venturing into Satan's territory. Our enemy will not readily relinquish the kingdoms of the world to become the kingdoms of our Lord. Satan's most effective strategy is not hostile religious worldviews, government restrictions, or persecution but his attack on the Christian worker. Succumbing to stressful situations and circumstances can bring discouragement, dissension, and defeat and render one ineffective in fulfilling one's calling and mission. *The Missionary Family: Managing Stress Effectively* is a valuable, practical tool in recognizing the enemy, staying focused on the task, and experiencing joy and fulfillment in one's calling.

Preface

I nearly died in 1979 from a rare combination of several stress-related diseases. Surviving by the grace of God, I began studying the nature of stress, its causes, effects, and treatments. Most of the material dealt with the medical and psychological aspects, but none mentioned the spiritual nature of stress management, nor did any of the works address the cross-linking of various causes, effects, and treatments. As a result, and at the request of church members who heard about my experience and studies, I developed a Christian Stress Management workshop that included many of the principles found in these pages. This workshop was presented in churches, a local college, and even at an association of medical workers. After a few years, however, I shelved the material and did not think about it for many years, until I nearly died again thirty years later in 2009, this time of a massive heart attack.

During the intervening years, I was blessed to serve as a missions administrator in two state conventions (Director of the Missions Department for the Tennessee Baptist Convention and Executive Director for the West Virginia Convention of Southern Baptists). God also has allowed me to travel to countries on six continents on nearly thirty short-term mission trips. I became friends with missionaries, mission agency leaders, and indigenous pastors.

Living and working with missionaries in North America and overseas, I became aware of the extremely stressful nature of their work, but I did not think to revisit my previous work in stress management until a regional conference of the Evangelical Missiological Society issued a call for papers regarding missionary families and their well-being. I found it necessary to restudy much of my previous work with investigation into more recent works and a much deeper study of God's Word than before.

After presenting a small paper on this subject at the conference, several people encouraged me to develop it into a book, the results of which you have in your hands. Not much has been written about stress on the mission field. The most recognized work is by Dr. Marjory Foyle, *Overcoming Missionary Stress*, which has been revised and republished under the title *Honorably Wounded: Stress Among Christian Workers*. I deliberately did not read Dr. Foyle's work until I had completed this book, not wishing to be influenced by another's material. We disagree on several points; however, hers is a study worthy of your consideration. We approach the subject from very different viewpoints, so readers would benefit from both works.

This book was not written from a desire to be published; I had already published five small books, and over two hundred articles and lessons with a total circulation exceeding 20 million. Rather, this work has the specific prayer that it will help missionary families in North America and around the world to cope with their extraordinary conditions on the mission field. If it helps reduce attrition of missionaries by even a fraction, it will be well worth the effort.

This book features **three distinctive approaches:**

1. It addresses not just the missionary, but the entire family. Often we who remain in the comfort of our homes forget that when a Christian worker moves to the mission field, an entire family goes along. These faithful believers are not just laborers but are husbands, wives, and children. Each has special needs and encounters unique stressors. Prayerfully every member of the family will find help as they serve the Lord. **Singles:** Families come in all shapes and sizes. A family of one, the single adult, can find help in this volume. Singles can discover principles that touch their lives and enhance their ministries.

2. It builds on the Word of God. This book finds its basis of truth, its epistemology, in Scripture. Throughout the work, you will see Scripture references, sometimes with the verse but often without. These notations are not merely given as proof-texts, but are offered with the hope you will open the Bible and read along. Only God's Spirit through God's Word can bring you to God's Son Who is the answer for all our needs, including handling the stressors of life.

3. It integrates causes, effects, and management methods with the five parts of human nature—the spirit, the body, and the soul (the soul includes our mind, will, emotions). One cannot separate the various elements of the human composition, for we are integrated, whole persons. Each area of the human being corresponds to various causes, effects, and management methods, which relate specifically to that area. At the same time, each part of a person affects each other part. Thus, a spiritual cause may have a physical effect. An emotional effect may have a management method related to the mind. So, this work attempts to integrate each of these areas as much as possible within our limitations.

Special Note: The examples found in this work represent composites of situations that missionaries experience. Names, locations, and other details have been changed so no individual might be identified with any portrayal. In addition, the writer does not claim to offer psychological counsel or medical advice. This book involves spiritual and practical observations based on Scripture, research, and experience. People suffering from severe stress should consult appropriate medical professionals.

CHAPTER ONE

Missionaries and Stress

"The stress became too much for us," Bill admitted when asked why he left the mission field.[1] Sadness crept over Bill's face as he recalled a series of problems encountered in his brief career as an international missionary.

In the days following glasnost and perestroika (openness and restructuring) at the collapse of the Soviet Union, Bill and Nancy responded to the call for workers in this newly opened country. Bill left a successful and comfortable pastorate in a small town to live in a large city where he and Nancy hoped to win many people for Christ.

Bill and Nancy tried to adapt to this dramatically different culture. They learned the language, ate the food, and lived in a small apartment a fraction of the size of their former home so they could be close to people. However, as they reached out to their neighbors, they were rebuffed. Bill couldn't understand why these people didn't realize their great need for salvation or why they refused the good news of Jesus. Moreover, Bill and his wife were overwhelmed by the hostility they encountered daily.

Nancy especially felt the brunt of culture shock and rejection. Trying to provide a semblance of normality in her home, she found it extremely difficult to find proper food and other needs in the shambles of an economy struggling to transform itself from socialistic communism to capitalism. After several years, the stress of daily life and the frustration of seeing few results from their labor took its toll. Bill and Nancy decided to return home.

The principles contained in this book can help reduce attrition and equip more missionary families for effective ministry. Obviously, any lasting solution for life and work must be found in Christ. These few pages have one goal—to point readers to the One Who can strengthen them and enable them to overcome the stressors they encounter. I pray that missionary families find help for their ministries and their family relationships.

Addressing Attrition

The story of Bill and Nancy is not unique. One large agency reported an annual loss of 4½ to 5 percent of its international force. With nearly 5000 missionaries, attrition involves between 200 and 250 people a year.

Common reasons missionaries give for departing the field include helping aging parents, providing children's education, or experiencing a change of call.[2] The first two problems involve normal developmental issues, but are nonetheless stressful, especially when missionaries are forced to choose between family responsibilities and the call of God to the field. Often the change of call may relate to burnout due to stress.

Another mission group experiences about 10 percent attrition among its American workers. This agency primarily uses national ministers in various countries for church planting and evangelism. Some missionaries leave the field because of stress but are reluctant to talk about it. Others who go home for a time overcome their difficulties and later return to their tasks. Another group transitions into other ministries. A few leave ministry completely.[3]

Should stress alone be enough to cause one to leave the mission field? We are inspired by stories of faithful saints who endured incredible suffering, yet remained on the field. In his book, *Lives Given, Not Taken*, Jerry Rankin, president emeritus of the International Mission Board of the Southern Baptist Convention, passionately records the stories of modern missionary martyrs. Each missionary chose to minister in dangerous settings and remained faithful to the end, making the ultimate sacrifice to reach people for Christ.

A few years ago, I had the privilege of speaking at the Carey Baptist Church in Calcutta, India. I was deeply moved by Carey's commitment to leave everything to follow God's call. His faithfulness in spite of obstacles inspired generations of missionaries. Names like Adoniram Judson and Luther Rice also come to mind as we consider pioneers who set the pace for international missions. Their missionary fervor touched thousands of lives and motivated countless missionaries to serve the Lord in distant places around the world.

During a visit to Westminster Abbey in London, I knelt by the tomb of David Livingstone and prayed, "Lord, give me a heart like this man." I had come from a mission trip to Malawi. Flying across the Zambian border, I looked down on the region where Livingstone's heart had been buried. He had instructed his followers to remove his heart after his death and bury it among the African people he loved so much.

Each of these extraordinary people endured pressures most Christians will never know. Yet, God's call and the people's need motivated them to remain faithful in spite of inordinate stress. Certainly, few of us find ourselves in the same categories of Carey, Judson, Rice, or Livingstone. Still, thousands of missionaries make the same commitments and, by God's grace, endure.

While ministering with a missionary couple in a difficult country, I learned that Sarah had developed cancer. This was her second episode with the deadly disease. I asked why she did not go back home where she could get

> *"I've found it does not matter where you die as long as you live in the will of God."*

better treatment. She replied softly, "I was born in one country among a lost family. Immigrating to the United States, I became a Christian and, then, a US citizen. God sent us to a third country where we served as missionaries for many years, and now we are here in this country. I've found it does not matter where you die as long as you live in the will of God."

Surviving Stress

Stress rarely reaches the level of threatening one's life. Paul wrote to the Hebrew people: "You have not resisted unto blood" (Hebrews 12:4). His comment referred to striving against sin, not staying true on the mission field. Yet, the application remains appropriate. Few Western believers experience such pressure in service to Christ that our lives are in danger. On the other hand, millions of Christians in the 10–40 Window and countless missionaries serving in restricted areas face opposition, imprisonment, expulsion, and even death as they proclaim Christ.

No one should judge the motives or the pressures others face as they serve the Lord on foreign fields. Nor should we second-guess faithful servants who return from the field. Missionaries should view the issues raised in this book not as excuses to leave the field, nor as remedies to remain. Instead, the following pages offer help in being more effective through understanding and managing the stressors missionary families experience daily.

Life on the mission field involves challenges, opportunities, and wonders. Yet, few careers involve as much exposure to stress as that of the missionary. Missionary families not only experience the normal developmental and circumstantial pressures of life, but they also encounter being uprooted from home, family, and friends. They generally learn a new language or two, wear different clothing, adapt to a foreign culture, and much more. Each change produces its own type of stress.

Many individuals manage stressors well; others suffer harmful effects of prolonged, unmanaged stress. Hans Selye, pioneer in stress management, described stress as the body's reaction to change.[4] Since human beings prefer homeostasis, any disruption to routine produces stress. Selye called this the General Adaptation Syndrome (GAS). His theory states the more life changes one experiences in a short period of time, the more stress one undergoes.

Psychologists Holmes and Rahe developed a life-change measurement that assigned incremental points to life changes. However, change alone cannot be a definitive measure of stress, since people react differently to various kinds of change. In the next chapter, we will discuss many of the variables related to individual responses to various stressors.

Missionaries tend to undergo more changes than the average person, contributing to larger degrees of stress in their lives. In addition, their families experience specific issues that go beyond reaction to changes. Problems such as pain (physical and emotional), trauma, injury and illness, and financial crises are common consequences of change. In addition, missionary families experience unique challenges, partly due to the cross-cultural nature of their environment, but more especially because of their task. Missionaries take the good news of Jesus to a world whose response ranges from shrugging indifference to open hostility.

Most missionaries surrender to the call to missions with enthusiasm. Because they are so excited about the prospect of nations of lost people hearing the gospel, they may assume that everyone will receive both it and them eagerly. That people may ignore, resist, or oppose the messengers and the message shocks and hurts them.

Missionaries deal with the stress of a resistant culture. We should not be surprised at people's opposition to the message of Christ and His messengers. Jesus said, "If the world hates you, you know that it hated me before it hated you. If you were of the world, the world would love his own: but because you are not of the world, but I have chosen you out of the world, therefore the world hates you. Remember the word that I said unto you, 'The servant is not greater than his lord.' If they have persecuted me, they will also persecute you; if they have kept my saying, they will keep yours also" (John 15:18–20). Even if one goes into a difficult situation with eyes wide open, knowing trouble is inevitable does not make it less troublesome.

This work seeks to describe the nature of stress in the context of the missionary family, whether serving in North America or internationally. It prayerfully offers a clearer understanding of some of the causes, effects, and management methods missionaries might experience. Its limited scope prevents an exhaustive study of either the missionary context or all the aspects of stress management. However, these few pages offer help to the missionary family struggling with stress.

Ultimately, the key to faithfulness on the mission field rests in heeding the admonition not to "fail of the grace of God" (Hebrews 12:15). Only in God's grace and strength can one respond to the call to missions, and only through Him can one remain true to that call. Prayerfully, this book will help missionaries and their families manage pressures in their lives and be more effective as they respond to God's grace.

A short cut through these pages would simply bring you to Jesus, for He alone gives peace: "Peace I leave with you, my peace I give unto you: not as the world gives, give I unto you. Let not your heart be troubled, neither let it be afraid" (John 14:27).

CHAPTER TWO

Understanding the Nature of Stress

S tress is not something that happens to people. People experience stress as a reaction to changing external circumstances, inner conflict, interpersonal relationships, sin, or other influences. Some changes are under our control. We choose to engage in certain behavior whose consequence produces pressure of one type or another. Other stressors are thrust upon us. Some stress is physiological in nature; at other times, it results from emotional trauma or spiritual failures.

Because human beings are like snowflakes (no two are completely alike), each individual responds differently to diverse stressors. When confronted with various challenges, some people experience varying levels of stress, while others use the situations to provide inner motivation for higher achievement.

To grasp concepts regarding stress, we must first apprehend the nature of the human being. Too often, counselors treat stressed persons primarily in terms of physical or emotional responses. Psychoanalysts may spend years with a client investigating childhood experiences, dreams, or responses to emotional trauma without approaching the real problems from a biblical position. Physicians often treat sufferers with various medications, attempting to elevate the mood, heal an ulcer, or moderate the blood pressure. Doctors rarely have the luxury of enough time to engage their patients in lengthy discussions about their life circumstances or the manner in which the patients have chosen to respond.

Sally appeared hyperexcitable, nervously talking and laughing simultaneously. Wanting something for her "nerves," she sought medication to help her calm down. Instead of improving, Sally's condition worsened, even harming her relationship with her husband. Seeking help from a Christian counselor, Sally revealed a series of life events and her reactions. The counselor suspected the stress in her life had become so overwhelming that Sally had become clinically depressed. With her permission, he spoke with her physician, not presuming to have medical knowledge, but sharing his suspicion. The doctor examined Sally, taking extra time to explore her emotional problems. As a result, he gave her a different medication. The drugs did not overcome her depression, but the partnership of a medical doctor and a Christian counselor helped Sally begin to deal with the real sources of her problems and find solutions that returned her to a normal, happy life.

A pill may be necessary to deal with a physical problem, but cannot resolve spiritual issues. Counseling may reveal emotional conflicts, but will not eliminate biological conditions that affect emotions. People are much more complicated. To understand the nature of stress, we have to consider the makeup of the human being.

The Human Composition

Theologians debate whether humans are dichotomous or trichotomous. Are people composed of two parts (body and soul; material and spiritual) or three parts (body, soul, and spirit)? (1 Thessalonians 5:23; Hebrews 4:12). Commonly, we understand the soul to involve the mind, will, and emotions. Some scholars argue that the terms *soul* and *spirit* refer to the same nonmaterial aspect of human nature. However, Scripture argues: "For the word of God is quick, and powerful, and sharper than any two-edged sword, piercing even to the dividing asunder of **soul and spirit**…" (Hebrews 4:12, emphasis added). The apostle Paul spoke of all three aspects of the human being: "And the very God of peace sanctify you wholly; and I pray God your whole **spirit and soul and body** be preserved blameless unto the coming of our Lord Jesus Christ" (1 Thessalonians 5:23, emphasis added).

From a practical viewpoint, one must deal with not two or three, but five aspects of human composition—mind, emotions, will, spirit, and body. Focusing on each part separately from the others fails to understand the integrated nature of the person. Any consideration of human health must involve a holistic approach, for each component affects the others.

The Soul—Dr. Charles Solomon argues that human beings are created souls. "And the LORD God formed man of the dust of the ground, and breathed into his nostrils the breath of life; and man became a living soul" (Genesis 2:7). He adds that these souls have bodies to relate to the physical world and spirits with which they relate to the spiritual world. Whatever affects one area of life influences the whole.[1]

Some stress may emanate from physical causes, but result in mental or emotional symptoms. How one behaves (the expression of the will) may proceed from what one thinks (the mind) or how one feels (emotions). The spiritual nature of persons impacts all other parts of life. Thus, stress management cannot be limited to one or two aspects of human design, but must integrate all of life—the spirit, the body, and the soul (mind, emotions, will).

The Mind—People develop patterns of thought and attitude early in life. Having a positive or negative outlook may be affected by personal decisions, family influences, and environmental conditions. Still, no one can excuse personal responsibility by blaming circumstances for stressful situations. Identical twins growing up in the same environment can exhibit widely different attitudes. More than the circumstances themselves, how we choose to react to life events contributes to our habits of thought.

Being able to solve problems and think through to good decisions can relate to intelligence related to biological or genetic sources. However, many people with average, or even below-average, intelligence quotients learn to make wise decisions through study of Scripture, seeking guidance from God's Spirit, gaining a good education, or personal reading and training.

Stress can relate to patterns of thought, attitudes, problem-solving abilities, and more. Mental processes can be sources of stress, offer evidence of unmanaged stress, or provide means for managing stress.

The Emotions—The Bible employs various ways of describing human emotions. We are angry, happy, fearful, joyous, peaceful, and anxious. The Bible sometimes uses the heart, the bowels, and the reins (kidneys) as metaphors to describe the source of emotions. Emotions can be a barometer of one's health. "A joyful heart is good medicine, but a broken spirit dries up the bones" (Proverbs 17:22). Some emotions surge forth involuntarily. For example, Joseph was overcome with emotions when he saw his long, lost younger brother (Genesis 43:30). At the same time, we have some control over how we express emotions. We can be angry, but choose to handle it in such a way as not to sin. "Be angry and sin not, let not the sun go down on your wrath" (Ephesians 4:26). We can choose not to be anxious (Psalm 37:1–8). We can decide to rejoice (1 Thessalonians 5:16).

Emotions relate directly to our experience with and expression of stress. People who tend to be emotionally expressive may exhibit stronger feelings when under stress. They may be louder verbally, cry more easily, get angry more quickly, or become afraid more readily. Other personalities may feel various emotions just as strongly, but internalize them, often with more serious impact to themselves and others.

The Will **(behavioral issues)**—Scripture refers to the human will in many ways. The term itself is rarely used except in reference to God's will: "And the world passes away, and the lust thereof: but he that doeth the will of God abides forever" (1 John 2:17). The Bible uses the term *flesh* to describe the internal nature of human beings that resists the influence of the Holy Spirit. More often, Scripture speaks of specific behaviors as reflective of the results of human will.

Behavior remains the best primary way to observe the nature of the will. Not only what we do but what we choose not to do emerges from decisions of the will. Behavior includes not only our actions but our speech. What we say and how we say it can bring peace or produce conflict. "And the tongue is a fire, a world of iniquity: so is the tongue among our members, that it defiles the whole body, and sets on fire the course of nature; and it is set on fire of hell" (James 3:6). On the other hand, speech can edify, exhort, and encourage. What we choose to say and how we say it reveals our hearts (will).

The Spirit—God made human beings in His image. God is Spirit and that which differentiates human beings from animals is the fact that people have spirits. As spiritual beings, we are drawn intuitively to God and cannot be truly satisfied except in Him. In mankind's natural state, however, our spirits are dead; they exist but need regeneration in order to be complete again (Ephesians 2:1–5).

Lost persons especially have difficulty overcoming stress or any other problem because their spirits exist, but are inert—dead in sin and trespasses (Ephesians 2:1). Thus, they are unable to relate properly to God or spiritual matters (1 Corinthians 2:14). Salvation involves the regeneration of the human spirit. The Holy Spirit of God comes to indwell the believer as we are saved, "Not by works of righteousness which we have done, but according to his mercy he saved us, by the washing of regeneration, and renewing of the Holy Ghost" (Titus 3:5).

God's Spirit bears witness to our spirit that we are His children (Romans 8:16). Being saved does not eliminate problems, nor does conversion insure success over stress. However, believers have the person of the Holy Spirit indwelling, empowering, sealing, and guiding them. Through God's grace, Christ's atonement, and the Spirit's presence and power, every believer can experience victory over sin, stress, and other adversities.

> *Through God's grace, Christ's atonement, and the Spirit's presence and power, every believer can experience victory over sin, stress, and other adversities.*

The Body—Our bodies are the net result of genetic inheritance from parents, grandparents, other ancestors, plus environmental influences and our personal choices. Some people are genetically more resistant to stress than others. Susceptibility to various illnesses, such as heart disease and cancer, as well as vulnerability to other stress-related diseases may relate to the collective chromosomes passed down from our families. Environmental factors include availability of good nutrition, health care, pollution, and economic status. Someone born in poverty is less likely to be healthy and may have serious physical problems.

Human beings' physical nature not only relates to one's biological and genetic makeup but to what one does with the body. Engaging in healthy physical activity aids resistance to stress. Healthy diet and consistent exercise contribute to the body's ability to handle stressful situations. On the other hand, a lifetime of eating food full of fats and sugar, combined with a sedentary lifestyle, produces an unhealthy body and, often, a sluggish mind. Similarly, work and sleep habits powerfully affect one's physical well-being.

An Integrated Approach to Understanding Stress

Good Stress? Not all stress is bad. Eustress (good stress) is vital to human well-being. Dr. Robert Eliot observes that when engaged in challenges, success produces a sense of well-being as healthy endorphins are released and levels of harmful hormones decrease.[2] Missionaries who lead someone to Christ sense tremendous elation. Their joy on a spiritual level produces a positive physical and emotional response. Long hours invested in reaching the person are like birth pangs, which are forgotten once the new babe in Christ is delivered (John 16:21). In a different scenario, some people need the motivation of deadlines to focus on certain tasks. While deadlines are stressful if time is not well managed, the satisfaction of completed work can be almost euphoric.

The Biological Side of Stress. God designed people to respond to life situations. When encountering danger, adrenaline provides quick reflexes, pupils dilate to see clearer, and the heart rate increases, providing more blood to the brain and muscles. Selye called this initial reaction the Alarm stage.

During the alarm stage, when one encounters a stressful situation, the body produces additional cortisol and epinephrine. Cortisol stimulates energy production and oxygen levels. It also affects the heart, brain, and muscles. Epinephrine is also a neurotransmitter. On the short term, the stress reaction aids our ability to handle emergencies. However, if stress is chronic and intense, these reactions can negatively affect the body. Cortisol, secreted during stress, has an especially harmful effect on heart tissue when incessant stress promotes too much of the hormone.[3]

Problems begin when the stress-causing situation, or our reaction to it, continues into the **Resistance stage**. Selye calls this experience "distress." The American Medical Association notes that "as stresses accumulate, an individual becomes increasingly susceptible to physical illness, behavioral and emotional problems, and injuries."[4] Mayo Clinic physicians observe that sustained stress can suppress the immune system, increasing susceptibility to disease. It can also lead to asthma, gastrointestinal problems, chronic pain, arthritis, fibromyalgia, mental disorders, and other issues.[5]

If extreme stress, or uncontrolled reaction, continues, exhaustion (depression, illness, even death due to heart attack or stroke) can ensue. The idea of burnout identifies this tertiary **Exhaustion stage** of stress reaction. Symptoms include pessimism, a sense of meaninglessness, and feelings of hopelessness.[6] At this point, some people resort to suicide to escape their pain. Teens may engage in cutting, self-mutilation, or other self-destructive actions. Some commentators suggest that young John Mark may have succumbed to stress overload when he left the first missionary journey and returned home (Acts 13:13). Overwhelming, unmanaged stress can prematurely end a God-called ministry.

Where does stress come from? Stress can be endogenous or exogenous. Exogenous stress relates to circumstances external to the individual. Situations, events, and crises afflict everyone at various times. Externally caused stress can be relieved by dealing with the cause or adjusting to the changing situation. Endogenous stress may relate more to physiological problems (such as genetic predispositions or physical illness) or to mental and emotional difficulties. Evidence of endogenous stress includes unrealistic expectations, perfectionism, chronic worry, negative attitudes, and irresponsible behavior.[7] Endogenous stress may require medical assistance or the aid of a Christian counselor.

So what do we do about it? In this study, we will observe spiritual, mental, emotional, behavioral, and physical aspects of the human being as related to the causes, effects, and management methods of stress. As we have already mentioned, each aspect of human nature interacts with the others.

Spiritual causes may have mental or emotional effects. Emotional causes may have physical effects. Physical causes may have mental or behavioral effects.

Sufferers may need a composite plan involving spiritual actions (including forgiving, trusting, loving, hoping), physical steps (like exercise, relaxation, diet, or medical help), emotional restructuring (such as gaining control of anger and replacing fear or worry with hope), mental reeducation (transforming the way one views life and solves problems as the Holy Spirit guides one into truth through Scripture), or behavioral habits (like deciding to act according to biblical, Spirit-directed ways instead of living in the flesh).

Not All Stress Is Equal. The variety of human responses makes measuring stress difficult. Just as people have different pain thresholds, even so, they react to stress uniquely. Two people might encounter the same situation, but one experiences distress while the other engages with eagerness. Moving to a foreign country might be an exciting adventure to some members of a missionary family, but stressful to others.

Consequently, the issue is not the amount of stress, but the amount of *unmanaged stress* one experiences that can be problematic. Studies indicate that as many as 20 percent of the population are "hot reactors" who overreact to what should be normal or unstressful situations.[8] Instead of taking challenges in stride, everything becomes a crisis. Such individuals maintain a high level of stress hormones, negatively affecting them physically, emotionally, and potentially spiritually.

Professor Richard Ecker, in his book *The Stress Myth*, argues that our perceptions of the situations, not the problems themselves, are sources of stress.[9] Some people react to major life changes as life or death crises. They can be so hampered emotionally they fail to engage properly in problem solving to deal with the changes. Others see the same experience as an opportunity for a new adventure. Conversely, while small annoyances are hardly noticed by some personality types, others react to constant petty problems as if they were experiencing water torture. Each person needs to understand how he or she responds to various types of situations and develop stress-resistant habits to manage each change successfully.

Factors Influencing Reaction to Stress

Spirituality

One's relationship with Christ is the most important factor in perceiving and reacting to stress. As discussed later in this work, someone who experiences the Spirit-filled life faces stressful life situations with more faith, hope, and love than others. Such a person responds to problems differently because spiritual resources provide inner capabilities for overcoming distressful events. The apostle Paul was able to be content with being either in difficult situations or in happy circumstances because of Christ who strengthened him (Philippians 4:11–13).

Some people consider missionaries to be super-Christians. They assume that anyone who will leave family, friends, and familiar surroundings to minister to unbelievers must have a special relationship with the Lord. Indeed, missionaries have obeyed God's call out of personal commitment to Him. Still, missionaries have the same need for personal spiritual development as other believers. They face similar, and in some cases superior, temptations. They struggle to make time for private spiritual devotions. They wrestle with anger, fear, envy, and other types of emotions just like anyone else.

Whether on the mission field or in the comfort of one's home, as believers, we must choose to develop our personal spiritualities. If we neglect our walk with Christ and disregard our need for personal devotions, we are left to respond to problems in the frailty of the flesh. On the other hand, cultivating the Spirit-filled life enables believers to face challenges with the power of God.

Attitude

Stress-resistant people tend to have positive attitudes toward life. Their glass is half full instead of half empty. Their clouds have silver linings. Their world is controlled by a loving heavenly Father who cares for them and is active in their lives. Some persons are naturally positive due to personality type, parental influence, environmental advantages, or other factors. Others have learned to cultivate attitudes of faith under the tutelage of Scripture, guided by the Holy Spirit, and encouraged by godly parents, friends, and other influences.

On the other hand, people whose first response to change is negative have a more difficult time with stress. They expect worst-case outcomes rather than believing God for better results. Perhaps they have suffered more difficulties or trauma in life than others. Pain tends to breed wariness of whatever threatens to inflict more pain. Other people simply have assumed cynical, jaded attitudes toward life. They view the world around them as hostile and believe they must constantly protect themselves and their loved ones from harm. Instead of enjoying a life of faith, they suffer from various levels of fear that often hide just beneath the surface of their awareness before leaping forth when stressful circumstances inevitably appear.

Personality Type
Categories of Personalities

Personality types account for some variation of stress reaction. Typical categories include Type A or Type B behaviors. Type A persons are often driven, task oriented, and high energy. They tend to be demanding of themselves and others and easily fall into workaholic lifestyles. Their encounters with other people can be brusque and may be viewed as arrogant and self-centered.

Type B personalities incline toward being easygoing and low-key. They often are people oriented and love group interaction, even taking a secondary role in relationships in order to find acceptance by others. They generally are patient, enduring, and quiet.

However, people are more complicated than these classifications. One cannot simply place oneself or others in a personality pigeonhole. Nor does personality alone determine stress interaction.

Another approach to personality typology is the DISC method, originally developed by William Marston and popularized through the work of John Geier. While understanding all people have some of each factor, the four letters describe distinct aspects of personality. D represents dominance. The D personality tends to be task oriented, proactive, aggressive, and bottom-line driven. The D thinks in bullet points, dislikes small talk, and loves challenges. The I (influencer) personality is outgoing and people oriented, wants to be liked, and cares more about social interaction than task accomplishment. The S (steady) personality loves low-key, easygoing, people-intensive group activity. This person dislikes sudden change, preferring the safety of familiar routine. The C (conscientious) personality is cautious, analytical, passively task oriented, and desirous of facts and order.

Responses to Stress

Each personality approaches stress differently. Some people enjoy a challenge and embrace change (as long as they initiate it) but get stressed by what they consider pettiness. Other personalities experience stress when their conclusions are challenged. A third group accepts change as an opportunity to meet new people. However, if the change involves conflict, some types become stressed. Perhaps the most stress-resistant personality is the naturally low-key person who does not get overwrought easily. These individuals generally maintain strong support groups to help when challenges occur. At the same time, they react negatively to rejection and pressure.

Conflicting Interactions

The various personality types can have adverse reactions on each other in a family or work context. Driven personalities may view people-oriented personalities as shallow and perceive their need for social interaction as a waste of time. This person may see low-key personalities as lacking motivation and initiative. Dominant personalities can experience conflict with conscientious types who ask many questions about procedure and accuracy of facts.

People-oriented personalities may consider dominant ones to be arrogant, inconsiderate, and bullying in nature. At the same time, they get along well with laid-back personalities because they like to talk, while the others enjoy listening. Quality-control personalities and people-oriented personalities can experience conflict because the latter likes to engage on a personal basis, while the former prefers remaining impersonal.

When persons with conflicting personality type interact, they may inflict stress on each other unless they recognize their need for each another. When each realizes that God made every person with traits that help other people be more complete, and when all have godly love toward one another, various personality types become positive enhancements to personal growth and inter-personal engagement.

Viva La Difference!

Understanding personality types not only help us understand ourselves, it aids our perceptions of other people. Conflicts can be avoided and communication enhanced by applying knowledge of personality interactions. Relationships are further enhanced when families, colleagues, or other groups not only understand each other's personality characteristics but appreciate their need for each other's distinctiveness.

Mission teams, families, and other groups need task-oriented personalities to keep them moving forward toward goal accomplishment. Low-key, group-oriented persons help provide cohesiveness of team spirit and group effort. People-focused individuals help everyone to be sensitive to people issues. Persons with conscientious tendencies encourage others to consider all the facts and follow all the rules. Each type is valuable to the other types. Just as God gives members of the church different spiritual gifts, which combine to fill all the needs of the Body, even so He brings people of various personality types together for each other's benefit.

Test to Know Your Style

Each person's makeup involves a certain amount of each of these personality types. The combinations are numerous. Several testing instruments are available in print and online that can help you identify your particular personality profile. At the same time, one should be careful employing do-it-yourself analyses. Without proper training, misinterpretation and misapplication of results may do more harm than good. Most missions agencies have member care personnel who are capable of administering various instruments and can help workers and their families understand themselves and one another better.

Several testing instruments (such as the Taylor-Johnson Temperament Analysis) integrate personality and temperament qualities. Simple tests result in composite graphs demonstrating behaviors on scales between nine opposite traits, such as nervous versus composed, or depressive as opposed to light-hearted.[10] The Myers-Briggs Type Indicator (MBTI) analysis is another testing instrument. However, each of these inventories tends to focus on secular psychological theories as opposed to scriptural foundations. While such instruments can be helpful to a degree, one should be wary of any approach that does not find its epistemology in the Word of God.

Temperament

A corollary aspect of human personality is **temperament**. Popularized by Tim LaHaye's book, *Spirit-Controlled Temperament*, temperament typology focuses on emotional orientation. Choleric temperaments tend to be short tempered and demanding. Melancholic types often become introspective and worrisome. Phlegmatic persons may take life as it comes with subdued reactions to problems. Sanguine temperaments appear to be happy-go-lucky types who enjoy life. As with personality types, individuals have a mixture of temperaments and no person is solely one type or another.[11]

Related to stress reactions, persons with choleric temperaments tend to react to stressful situations aggressively, intending to overcome the problem by force of will. Melancholic types are often introspective, constantly brooding over problems (or perceived problems) with worried minds and fearful hearts. Sanguine individuals may seem to be the most stress-resistant temperament types since they appear to be energetic, happy, and engaging. However, their emotional expressions often cover hidden insecurities that flare under pressure, especially when they sense personal rejection. Phlegmatic persons range from relaxed to apathetic in their response to life. Some may simply shrug off stressful challenges; others may seem self-controlled, but experience inner turmoil that can have serious consequences if it goes on unknown and unchecked.

On a more positive note, each temperament type has certain strengths in handling stress. The choleric individual may handle more serious stress with greater assurance than other types. Phlegmatic persons rarely allow small stress to get under their skin, but see matters in levelheaded perspective. Sanguine people engage life with a cheerful, optimistic attitude. While definitely challenged due to their tendency toward sadness, melancholic temperaments may have certain strengths in approaching problems thoughtfully and analytically.

Ministers interested in studying personality and temperament types and their interactions from a biblical standpoint can find many illustrative examples in Scripture. Paul, for example, was strong willed yet loving, willing to be confrontational yet conciliatory. He was able to reason intellectually but was not dependent solely on rational arguments for belief and doctrine. Barnabus was an encourager of the brethren who looked for opportunities to lift up others. James remained strong in Jewish ethics and behavior, wanting to insure correct obedience to God's will while responding to the grace of Christ. Andrew, kind and approachable, was always encountering other people and bringing them to Jesus.

Whether considering personality or temperament types, we cannot simply excuse inappropriate behavior with the attitude of the comic character Popeye: "I am what I am and that's all that I am." God enables us to be and do more than our basic natures suggest. When filled with His Spirit, the fruit of the Spirit is freed to flow through believers' lives: love, joy, peace, patience, gentleness, goodness, faith, and self-control. Through His enablement, we can be better than we were and respond to stressful situations with overcoming faith and quiet hearts.

Learned Reactions

Another variable involves **learned reactions**. Through experience and education, people adapt their responses to stressors. Although their basic nature, upbringing, or culture may be disposed to certain reactions, they can adjust to manage stress more effectively. For example, a person who has had a heart attack after a lifetime of poor diet, bad genetics, and hard-driving work habits can learn to eat better, manage time more effectively, and use new medications that can help with genetic issues such as high cholesterol.

On the other hand, some people allow hurtful situations to shape their attitudes and actions into negative patterns, resulting in more serious stress formations. Growing up in dysfunctional, painful environments, some persons learn to overcome problems with aggression, while others may withdraw physically or emotionally. Constant infliction of pain can create scars that influence how one reacts to potentially harmful conditions.

We cannot blame our environment, experiences, or other people for how we respond to life challenges. However, by understanding how patterns of reaction have formed, we can be transformed through the Holy Spirit's renewal of our minds and hearts (Romans 12:2).

Gender

Increasingly, females suffer stress-related illnesses once thought to be unique to males. They have many demands, such as childcare and household responsibilities associated with traditional roles. However, growing percentages of women follow career tracks with significant stress in the workplace, adding to levels of stress typical to their gender roles. Consequently, stress has become one of the foremost health problems among women.[12]

Stress has become one of the foremost health problems among women.

Women tend to react differently to stress than do men. Obviously, females vary between one another based on different criteria, but women in general have certain commonalities. Edward Charlesworth and Ronald Nathan argue that women are twice as likely as men to suffer from depression, especially due to events that isolate them from normal relationships, including death, divorce, and an empty nest. In addition, females are more likely to care for sick family members or elderly parents.[13]

Kevin Leman, in his book, *The 6 Stress Points in a Woman's Life*, lists **six key areas of stress in women's lives**:

1. Children
2. Time
3. Husbands
4. Money
5. Housework
6. Career[14]

Consider each of these issues as related to married women on the mission field:

Child rearing in normal circumstances places tremendous stress on mothers. On the mission field, women's loads can become even heavier. The absence of nearby family to help with childcare and nurturing, the lack of adequate medical resources, and isolation from other families with children of like ages affects mothers' stress. With missionary husbands away from home due to work-related travel, moms often must provide both discipline and nurturing—a difficult balance.

Time demands also create extra burdens on missionary wives. They not only have the normal issues of household management, raising children, and, possibly, handling a job outside the home, but they also sense responsibility in the ministry itself. They are called to be missionaries as much as their husbands. Desiring to make a difference, they get involved in personal witnessing, Bible studies with other women, leading various ministries in the church, and many other activities. Balancing the time requirements challenges the most capable of persons. Stress inevitably occurs as various needs demand simultaneous attention.

Husbands must recognize the added stress and work to avoid adding to it. Understanding spouses encourage their wives by affirming them in small, as well as large, ways. Being sensitive to what and how one speaks can deter conflict and avoid hurt feelings. Men can find ways to help with the children and the house. They need also to see their wives as co-laborers and not make the mistake of treating wives as surrogate secretaries on the field. By ministering to their wives and children, men can help relieve their stressful burdens and insure the entire family experiences a happier environment.

Financial concerns affect both men and women, but often fall on wives' shoulders more heavily when busy husbands delegate household management to them. Few missionary families have enough money to meet all their needs. Many missionaries use personal funds to supplement ministry budgets and assist needy people they encounter. Trying to decide how to allocate limited resources strains an already stressed missionary wife, often beyond the limits. Husbands and wives must see themselves as partners in fiscal responsibility, with each bearing appropriate roles in handling family business matters.

Housework, demanding on its own, becomes even more stressful when the missionary wife tries to manage secular employment at the same time. Many missionary families have found local helpers who can be hired to aid in cooking, cleaning, child care, and other needs. At the same time, sensitivity has to be used so local nationals do not perceive the missionary as being rich, while they themselves are relegated to a servant class.

Summary of Stress Variables

Each of these variables affects the degree to which people are able to manage stress. What may seem like a trivial matter to one person can be the proverbial straw that broke the camel's back for another. No single variable determines the degree of stress resilience people might have. Combinations of all the various factors are nearly infinite.

Of greatest importance, individuals' spiritual maturity affects reaction to any and all of these influences. By understanding our personal makeup and environment, we can more effectively cooperate with the Holy Spirit in handling components of life with grace, peace, and strength. As Paul expressed in his epistles, "Grace be to you and peace from God the Father, and from our Lord Jesus Christ" (Galatians 1:3).

CHAPTER THREE

Understanding the Missions Context

In addition to the normal sources of stress in daily life, missionary families encounter unique situations that add to their potential for stress-related problems. Certainly, every vocation—from the military to the ministry, from the farm to the factory, from Wall Street to Main Street—has special circumstances producing distinctive difficulties. Our focus, the missionary family on the field, combines many of these situationally specific issues and adds its own complications.

Answering the Call

Most people don't wake up one day and decide to be a missionary. Missionaries sense a unique call of God. The process of the call can be stressful since it involves sacrifice and change. The thought of starting a new life in a strange place can be daunting at best. Only the sure sense of divine initiative can overcome the human inclination to remain in the safety of the familiar.

God's call summons many ministers with unmistakable clarity. Others struggle, some in knowing and others in yielding. Some people surrender to God's call with eagerness; others yield after years of doubt and questioning. The call may come through quiet contemplation or in the heat of service.

God's call to the mission field does not involve merely the husband or the wife; it affects the whole family and, thus, requires acknowledgment and acceptance by everyone involved. Unfortunately, some dominant men (or women for that matter) may claim God's call as their basis for uprooting their families and forcing a move to the mission field regardless of the reactions of the spouse or children. When the entire family does not embrace a call to the field, resistance and stress likely follow.

Our understanding of the call substantially influences how we respond to stress on the field. Some missionary families go with the intention of spending the rest of their lives in missions. They may move from field to field, but few problems are strong enough to deter them from their overall commitment to missions. On the other hand, some ministers see their call as more temporary in nature. They go without a vision of a lifetime on the field, but see themselves serving for a few years before coming back home to a different kind of ministry. Only God and the missionary family can judge the nature and extent of the call. However, people who lack a lifelong commitment are more likely to succumb amidst the stresses of service.

Leaving and Cleaving

When people leave their families of birth and marry, they cleave to (join with) each other in a new family of their own. Similarly, when missionary families go to a mission field, they experience the stress of leaving and cleaving. They leave families, friends, and familiar surroundings. Gone are the climates and culture they have known. Absent are the joyful sounds and delightful smells of holidays with the family. Distant are the hugs, smiles, and encouraging glances just when you need them. Technology, such as Skype, helps, but you can't easily hug a computer screen.

Houses have to be sold, furniture left behind, and accumulated items of a lifetime sorted to see what will fit into a moving crate. Not being able to transport material possessions may seem insignificant, but each item carries an emotional connection to the past. Leaving memories behind often breeds various grief responses, triggering stress.

Equally stressful is the adjustment to new people in a new place. Many countries use different voltage of electricity and different connections.

The family must leave behind appliances, entertainment devices, and other electrical machinery and purchase new equipment, adding to financial stressors. Going to a store not only involves a communication challenge but a lifestyle change in availability of foods, mentally recalculating sizes of clothes, understanding money exchange rates, and a hundred other problems. Accessing health care for a sick child when no doctor lives within easy access, finding medicine in a small village, or dealing with insects, temperature, and other discomforts all produce stress.

After establishing a new household, the missionary family faces the stress of making new relationships with their target people. The existence of an established group of churches can be helpful or may present obstacles that must be overcome. The absence of congregations means the work begins without a foundation of faith among nationals. On the other hand, an established ecclesiastical hierarchy could resist the missionaries and their strategies. Whatever situation a missionary encounters, stress follows.

Establishing Patterns of Life

People back home often imagine missionaries as having fascinating lives in exotic locations. However, after the initial adaptation to the local culture, most families settle down to basic regimens. Their days involve the same kinds of activities as their stateside counterparts—education for the children, work for the adults, preparing meals, cleaning clothes and homes, and the general habits of life.

Ironically, one of the great challenges of many mission fields involves the constant battle with boredom. Books and DVD movies, when they can be found, provide limited entertainment. Dependable high-speed Internet is not available in many missions' locations or can be very expensive. Social life generally focuses on family, interaction with other expatriates, or fellowship with church people or individuals being cultivated for witnessing opportunities.

In many cases, the father/husband missionary fills his days (and nights) with his work. The myriad of demands and opportunities challenge him, motivate him, and invigorate him. Other than school or shopping, the wife and children may lack opportunities for purposeful interaction with others on a daily basis. Tedium may gradually grate on everyone's nerves, slipping stress quietly into the family's life.

Isolation

Loneliness can be a major problem with missionary families. Isolation may be the result of living in remote locations, separated from other missionaries, or even other believers, by many hours of difficult travel. Isolation also occurs in urban areas with large populations. Whether serving internationally or domestically, missionaries may live and work among thousands of people, but have few friends.

A missionary's wife confided in a coworker, "I am so lonely." She and her husband worked in a North American mission field. They did not have to overcome barriers of language or other major cultural issues. They lived in a small city with thousands of people. Yet, she was nearly overwhelmed by the stress of isolation.

In her family's case, challenging geography, lack of adequate finances to travel, and a busy work schedule prevented regular visits with other missionaries. Missionary wives had even fewer occasions to see one another. Although the local region had several churches, the pastors' wives stayed busy with children and church demands. The missionaries had left family and friends to help in this domestic mission field whose population was over 80 percent unchurched. With few friends, especially without a close confident, this missionary wife was nearly at the breaking point.

Yes, many missionaries are outgoing and comfortable with initiating relationships. Other workers are more reserved and socially shy. Their families have the same dilemma. Social needs affect God's workers and their families just as much as anyone else. Dedication to the work does not eliminate the need for social interaction. Relationships provide vital support systems as well as vehicles for ministry. Without a network of close friends, missionaries and their families lack a listening ear and comforting shoulder in stressful times. "A friend loves at all times, and a brother is born for adversity" (Proverbs 17:17).

Balancing Time Demands

Without an accountability structure, people in ministry may be tempted to misuse that nonrenewable resource known as time. Consulting with a church planter in a northeastern American state, I was asked how to improve his productivity. The church was not growing as anticipated, resulting in discouragement for the minister and frustration for the church. When asked how he spent his time, he described a week in which he spent mornings at home studying. By mid-afternoon, he was home to help with the children, although his wife did not work outside the home. He was at church on Sunday mornings and Tuesday nights but otherwise was at home. We had discovered his problem! Without someone to set expectations and establish accountability, he had fallen into a pattern of not using time effectively.

Most missionaries have the opposite problem. They are diligent in their duties, faithful with their families, conscientious regarding their church, and usually need more hours in the day and more days in each week! One mission strategist estimated an effective church planter must make forty to sixty contacts per week to reach an unchurched community. Personal work among unreached people often requires time away from home, creating inner conflict for the missionary whose children are growing up with an absentee parent.

Administrative responsibilities often force the missionary to forego ministry tasks related to evangelism, disciple making, strategic development, or organizational needs. The typical worker may experience actual or perceived pressure from supervisors, local believers, governmental agents, and family members. Where does one find time to meet all the conflicting demands? Wise missionary families study time-management techniques to improve stewardship of time and relieve time-related stress.

Interacting with Culture (Shock)

Being a missionary usually involves adapting to another culture. Whether one serves in North America or internationally, workers generally leave familiar territory to engage unreached people whose customs, language, and even food differ from their own. Immersion in a new culture creates constant challenges for the missionary family. Instincts of self-preservation tempt them to cocoon themselves physically or emotionally, straying out into the culture only when absolutely necessary. One evangelistic worker in Central Asia found housing that allowed complete separation from the cacophony of noise and nastiness that pervaded the city. Trips into ministry venues grew increasingly few as the retreat offered relief from cultural stress.

Even missionaries who love their new culture experience stress. Changes require adaptations that can become stressors. Learning a new language comes easier to some, while being more difficult for others. Different kinds of foods means not only having to adapt one's palate, but gaining skill in using unusual ingredients to make unfamiliar meals. Clothing from one's homeland stands out on the mission field as if neon lights flashed above missionaries saying, "FOREIGNER!" What one may intend as a compliment or well-intended gesture may have very negative connotations in one's new society. Change results in stress which each person, children as well as adults, must learn to manage.

Interpersonal Relationships

An item on your childhood report card from school may have read something like this: "Plays well with others." Some people interact with others freely and naturally. They love to talk and rarely seem to meet a stranger. Others are more quiet and reserved, yet maintain positive relationships within their mission team and with people on the field. Being able to play, and work, well with others remains a key requirement of any worker, but it is especially important on the mission field.

Interpersonal relationships not only reveal themselves in social engagements, but in the work environment. Missionaries generally are not very effective unless they are proactive self-starters. However, that quality can become a detriment if not tempered by a humble spirit and willingness to cooperate with others. Missionaries may be isolated from one another due to far-ranging assignments; yet, they remain interdependent in many ways. They need both the attitude and the skills conducive to positive relationships.

Strategic Development

Some agencies rely on the field missionary to develop effective strategies for their assigned areas. Other groups establish standards based on the philosophical and theological values of agency leaders, requiring workers to model their plans after the general mandate. Both approaches produce stress, although of differing types. Working with other missionaries in one's agency to create a workable plan requires varying skills related to research, analysis, consolidation, long-range planning, and evaluation. Missionaries must be open to the give-and-take nature of group dynamics to arrive at a plan to which everyone can commit. Some workers enjoy activities related to research and analysis, while other missionaries just want to get on with the work. The paradoxical nature of mission work is independent, yet interdependent. When various workers are matched with their giftedness and interests, the entire process moves forward with much less stress.

Management and Administration

Every missionary is an administrator to one degree or another. A few workers have the specific responsibility of managing other missionaries, their logistical support, and the mission's strategic results. Agency structures help workers by compartmentalizing much of the administrative responsibilities. Workers with business backgrounds usually have the task of managing flow of funds, bookkeeping, governmental and legal matters, and reporting requirements.

Still, all missionaries must manage tasks, time, funds, facilities, and other elements of their work. Usually, missionaries receive some level of training in these and other skills before embarking on their work. In some cases, regardless of training, workers may experience stress in the daily requirements of administration. Clear, open, and honest communication between field workers and up-line administrators can reduce pressures and increase effectiveness of each level of management.

Working with Nationals

Rarely do missionaries engage unreached people groups alone. In most cases, some degree of Christianity already exists. Churches, pastors, and leaders, along with local and national ecclesiastic structures may greet the missionary with certain expectations. In other locations, the missionary may be the only believer within the target area. In both cases, missionaries must be well prepared with knowledge of the local people group, their customs and worldviews, and the general environment in which they live.

Some mission venues are harvest fields, yielding high results for effective work. Other people groups are more resistant to the gospel and remain nonreceptive toward foreign workers. Some cultures value rational logic and respond well to formal organization and structures. Other societies are more relational and informal by nature. Each group requires understanding and work approaches relative to their cultural patterns. Missionaries accustomed to well-organized plans, schedules, and order experience additional stress when operating among a more carefree people.

Being In and Under Authority

The nature of their calling and the position they hold give missionaries a certain amount of authority, both in their agencies and among local nationals. They are responsible to exercise authority in an effective, Christlike manner. Sometimes cultural differences cause unintended conflict when the missionary has to make decisions or direct activities that involve indigenous workers. Being sensitive to how each person perceives authority can help missionaries exercise leadership with a minimum of stress for everyone involved.

Sometimes, however, ministers must make judgments based on biblical principles and what is best for the overall work, even if such choices are not popular. Part of leadership involves a willingness to do what is right even if it results in criticism. Without being unnecessarily abrasive, leaders can be firm, yet loving. The question is not whether one has the authority to make decisions but how to exercise leadership with a servant's heart. The apostle Peter's advice to pastors makes wise application on the mission field:

"Feed the flock of God which is among you, taking the oversight thereof, not by constraint, but willingly; not for filthy lucre, but of a ready mind; neither as being lords over God's heritage, but being examples to the flock" (1 Peter 5:2–3).

At the same time, missionaries are under authority. They answer to regional leaders, agency administrators, and, ultimately, trustees. Some personalities resist others who exercise authority over them. Yet, while their ultimate authority is Christ, their temporal authority comes because they accept the authority above them. Jesus encountered such an attitude in the faithful centurion who understood authority comes by being under authority (Matthew 8:5–13).

The question is not whether one has the authority to make decisions but how to exercise leadership with a servant's heart.

Lack of Routine

Persons accustomed to regularity experience stress when confronted with the lack of routine on the mission field. Rarely are two days alike. While a semblance of order involves children's school schedules, church meetings, and monthly reports, the reality of missionary work varies greatly from week to week. Workers come to expect the unexpected as they engage people in an ever-changing environment. No one knows when the next crisis or opportunity will arise. The missionary may thrive on new challenges, but family members may tire of not seeing Dad and/or Mom at the dinner table regularly.

Helping the entire family understand the kind of routine, or lack thereof, they will experience on the field prepares them to make adjustments in expectations and habits. Instead of placing primary value on regularity of dinner together, for instance, the missionary family comes to appreciate the quality time when they are together. At the same time, missionaries need to make special efforts at providing the kind of lifestyle most conducive to a happy family and a successful ministry.

Communicating Here, There, and Yonder

Technology has enhanced the missionary experience greatly. Only a generation ago, missionaries relied on expensive phone calls or slow mail service to communicate with family, friends, supporters, and one another. With voice-over Internet protocol phone services, Skype and other video conferencing technologies, email and instant messaging, and other tools, missionaries are able to maintain communication easily and inexpensively.

Staying in touch with family back home, keeping contact with supporters (especially in cases of deputation-oriented agencies), and interacting with coworkers and mission administrators has never been more available. At the same time, the ease of communication can place additional strain on the missionary family. Constant calls from home remind them of what they're missing as birthdays and other special occasions pass without their being present. One missionary wife confided she loved being in touch, but found it time challenging to maintain relationships with friends and family back home while engaged in new friendships on the field.

The context of the mission field presents wonderful opportunities and unique challenges. The more families know about the various issues related to life on the field, the better prepared they will be to handle them. Stress is inevitable, but understanding yourself and the environment in which you will live and work can make the experience much more enjoyable and the work more successful.

CHAPTER FOUR

Evidence of Unmanaged Stress

One cannot really observe stress, only the results of unmanaged stress. As previously mentioned, people handle various kinds of potentially stressful situations according to a number of variables. When we say that someone is "stressed out," we generally have seen evidence of unmanaged stress. In preparing to counter stressors of life in general, and particularly on the mission field, we need to be able to recognize symptoms in ourselves and others.

Mayo Clinic physicians observe the following symptoms of unmanaged stress:

> **"Psychological (Mental/Emotional):** Anxiety, irritability, feeling of impending doom, depression, slow/racing thoughts, feelings of helplessness or hopelessness, sense of worthlessness, lack of direction, insecurity, sadness, defensiveness, anger, hypersensitivity, apathy

> **"Behavioral:** Overeating, loss of appetite, impatience, argumentative, procrastination, use of alcohol/drugs/ tobacco, withdrawal, isolation, neglecting responsibilities, poor job/school performance, burnout, poor hygiene, biting nails/pencils, less active, change in relationships/habits

"Physical: Headaches, grinding teeth, dry throat, clenched jaws, chest pain, shortness of breath, pounding heart, high blood pressure, muscle ache, indigestion, constipation, perspiration, cold/sweaty hands, fatigue, insomnia, frequent illness"[1]

The more frequent and numerous the effects, the higher degree of unmanaged stress likely exists. Because different people react differently to life changes, one of the best ways to determine the levels of personal difficulty they are experiencing remains observation of evidence of unmanaged stress. Problems generally occur not because a person undergoes a stressor, but as a result of not reacting well to it. Consequently, as stress continues unabated and unmanaged, family, friends, and coworkers may notice a growing accumulation of various effects from each of the categories.

Psychological Evidence

Psychological effects may be the first observable signs of stress that has become too hard to handle. Levels of anxiety and worry appear unusually common in such a sufferer. The person may demonstrate touchiness or ill temper toward friends and family members. A constant sense of sadness may surround the stressed-out believer, creating an attitude of always seeing the darker side of any situation and dampening any sense of joy or happiness. As stress continues unabated, sufferers may surrender to the lie that they are helpless to do anything about the problem, leaving them without hope.

Unmanaged stress can reveal itself in mental confusion, difficulty in concentration or decision making, and procrastination. Mental clutter from whatever conflict causes the stress can press so strongly on the consciousness that normal patterns of thought can be interrupted. Some people may become forgetful.

Doubt and distrust also disclose changes in patterns of thinking, which relate to unmanaged stress. As pressures build, adults and children alike can start wondering whether God really cares or whether God is actually present and involved in their lives. Just as the disciples questioned an awakening Jesus as they struggled with a sinking boat, we might be tempted to doubt God and His goodness. Distrust also affects relationships with other people, as stressed persons project their pain onto persons around them.

When unmanaged stress continues over an extended period, reinforced by a sequence of hurtful events, individuals may take on a negative outlook on life. Instead of seeing possibilities, they only see problems. Instead of opportunities, they envision obstacles. One stressful situation may cause them mentally to link future outcomes, usually with the worst-case scenarios being what they come to expect.

Emotionally, sufferers might wrestle with anger, worry, fear, or regret. They may swing from good moods to bad without evident cause. Sometimes little issues may become blown out of proportion and injure relationships, especially within the family. Overreactions should be understood not to be generated from specific incidents but from the accumulation of unmanaged stressors.

Children may complain of night terrors (nightmares). Such experiences often follow being threatened in some way, either in actuality or perception. Both are equally frightening to a child. Having to maintain a level of security or cover in restricted countries adds to the tension a child may sense. Parents should not dismiss these anxieties too quickly. Accepting the children's concern and helping them pray through their worries will help them confront and overcome the bad dreams and daily fears.

Behavioral Evidence

Accompanying the psychological effects are changes in behavior. Behavior reflects that component of human nature known as the will. Behaviors provide evidence of unmanaged stress. Missionaries, though motivated by the admirable desire to reach lost people, may find themselves unable to relax, often refusing holidays or vacations, and engaging in extreme multitasking. As stress mounts, they may begin to withdraw from associates, or even from their spouses. Some exhibit aspects of obsessive-compulsive behavior, feeling as if they must do certain things in specific, controlled ways.

Overeating or consuming the wrong foods can be one way stressed people compensate for their emotional discomfort. We often joke about stress causing us to eat high-carbohydrate comfort food. In reality, stressed people reach for their favorite junk food or whatever produces temporary relief from discomfort. Most missionaries would strictly avoid moral temptations when stress creates a deep hunger for some type of good feeling. However, overeating is a pleasure without apparent moral penalty. As weight gain changes their appearance, some sufferers begin to lose self-respect and worry if their physique will make them less attractive to their spouse, creating additional anxiety and stress.

Other behavioral changes may be noticeable in personal and interpersonal ways. Persons normally well groomed may begin to appear slovenly. Individuals who usually are open and friendly become reserved and withdrawn. Others appear uncooperative and even aggressive. Habits and mannerisms may change either gradually or abruptly, sometimes yielding to destructive tendencies.

Teens may act out in inappropriate ways. Adolescents who have been stable, obedient children could begin to engage in harmful, even sinful, activities. More than mere hormonal changes, this behavior may relate to an overwhelming burden of issues they have not been able to resolve. Grades plummet as they have less interest in studies. Participation in extracurricular activities may fall off when they struggle to maintain emotional equilibrium. Becoming increasingly isolated, they either ignore formerly close friends or reach out in inappropriate ways to receive peer approval and affection.

Children may also act out their stress at school or church. They may withdraw from friends and begin isolating themselves in their rooms. Some may extend their fears into their play activities. Unless parents recognize the symptoms and sensitively reach out with the ministry of prayer and presence, problems may escalate to unmanageable levels.

Physical Evidence

Effects on the body often occur as stress enters the resistance phase. The human body is amazingly resilient, but when it becomes overextended, unmanaged stress inevitably will affect one's physical well-being. Tension can produce constant headaches and other pain, sometimes resulting in using inordinate amounts of medication to manage the discomfort, creating additional problems. Physical effects include problems with the circulatory system as high blood pressure, faster heart rate, and chest pain occur.

These natural responses to stressors develop into dangerous combinations when the alarm stage moves into an ongoing resistance phase, putting demands on the body that can result in stroke or heart attack. Many gastrointestinal problems can be traced to unmanaged stress, including indigestion, reflux, ulcers, constipation, and colitis. Physicians point to prolonged stress as an underlying contributor to many illnesses as a person's resistance and immune system come under attack through the body's reaction to stress.

Ken woke up knowing something was wrong. The pain was different and greater than anything he had experienced before. He had suffered intensely stressful situations over a prolonged time. Feeling unable to change the conditions of his circumstances, he had merely endured—trying to put a good face on matters but inwardly experiencing churning emotions. Using inappropriate foods like double cheeseburgers to find a bit of pleasure and satisfaction, his weight had ballooned and, unknowingly, clogged a coronary artery. As the ambulance took him to the hospital, he did not immediately connect his failure to manage the stress with his present condition. He could only focus on enduring the pain.

Ken's story, unfortunately, merely presents one example of an all-too-familiar scenario among ministers. Overeating, lack of exercise, and unrelenting stress put a strain on bodies not intended for such abuse. Forgetting that their bodies are the temple of the Holy Spirit, they suffer the consequences.

Spiritual Evidence

Missionary families and other believers can experience spiritual effects of unmanaged stress. A crisis of faith may ensue. Martin Lloyd-Jones' book, *Spiritual Depression*, describes what he calls spiritual problems people experience, several of which could fit into this category of spiritual evidence of unmanaged stress.[2] Sometimes, missionaries recognize spiritual results of stress in themselves or their family members. If they serve for some time without seeing visible results or if they experience an ongoing crisis without resolution, they may begin to believe that God does not respond to their prayers.

Spiritual effects of unmanaged stress may include the following:

Reduced devotional life. People who experience spiritual depression may abandon or reduce frequency of quiet times. Not having regular communion with Christ often leads to other issues. One study indicates that a commonality of ministers who fail morally is the discontinuance of private time with God in prayer and Bible study. Without regular nourishment from the Word and consistent communication with the Lord, ministers lack the spiritual intake necessary for preaching, teaching, discipleship, and evangelism.

Bill was a prime example of what can happen when ministers abandon communion with Christ. Successful in many evangelistic efforts, Bill grew busier and busier. His travel schedule took him away from home constantly. Becoming stressed with the huge demands on his life, he ceased his regular devotional habits, believed he was too busy to retreat in prayer, and stopped studying the Bible. Weakened spiritually, he fell to a temptation involving an immoral relationship with a coworker. He lost his ministry and his family. Most of all, many people who had come to Christ through Bill's work were deeply wounded, with some even questioning their salvation because it involved a sinful minister.

Immersion in work. Believing their work is divinely ordained and salvation of a lost people group is urgent, many missionaries fall into patterns similar to workaholics. This spiritual problem mistakes self-effort for spiritual dynamic, revealing substitution of the works of the flesh for the fruit of the Spirit. The workers have good, even honorable, intentions. They are highly motivated by the overwhelming spiritual and physical needs around them. Desiring to see as many people as possible come to Christ, they may focus so much on the ministry that they do not minister to their own families. Neglecting even their own physical and spiritual needs, they fall prey to burnout.

Feelings of guilt or shame. Genuine guilt results from breaking God's commandments, operating in the flesh rather than the Spirit. Shame naturally results from conviction of sin, just as Adam and Eve were afraid and ashamed after their sin in the garden. They had not been ashamed of their nakedness during their innocence, but knowledge of evil as well as good caused them to flee the face of God (Genesis 2:25, 3:10). Genuine guilt and shame can only be relieved through genuine repentance and confession of sin. When God forgives, we no longer are subject to guilt, fear, and shame.

Stress can cause believers to question their forgiveness. Because they experience problems, they may assume God has not forgiven them. Satan's accusation and the natural inclination of the flesh to reflect constantly on failure can produce false guilt and shame. In this case, feelings of guilt have no specific object but remain vague and indefinable. Without specific sin to repent and confess, Christians have much more difficulty finding relief from false guilt and shame.

Lack of purpose. Extreme or consistent stress often accompanies failure to accomplish goals. Missionaries, like most ministers, often weigh their worthiness by success in ministry tasks. Believing, rightly so, in the eternal consequences of their work, falling short may cause them to question whether they should continue in the Lord's work. Stress can wear one down physically, emotionally, and spiritually, creating a weariness in well doing that results in a sense of spiritual wandering without purpose or direction. If they persevere, they not only will overcome any temporary sense of aimlessness, they will share in God's harvest (Galatians 6:9).

Charlie had a specific vision when he assumed leadership of a mission group in North America. He had wrestled with his call for nearly two weeks before accepting the invitation to lead the work in this northeastern state. When he had a clear idea of what God wanted him to do, he yielded to the call and immersed himself in the work. After three years of nonstop labor, and some degree of conflict, Charlie was approaching burnout. He had accomplished his original goals. Week after week, he went to the office and supervised activities and workers but lacked the kind of enthusiasm he once felt for the job. Increasingly he wondered if he should go somewhere else and try something new. Only when he began to manage the stress in his life through prayer and Bible study did he gain a fresh vision of the next phase of ministry and a renewed commitment to the task.

Feeling worried or afraid. Consistent worry or fear reveal one's attitude toward God. Instead of experiencing rest-producing faith in a God Who loves and cares for us, stressed persons exhibit persistent anxiety. They depend on self-effort instead of relying on a loving Father for whatever needs they encounter (Matthew 6:25–34). Consequently, they obsess with current and potential problems, unmet needs, and unresolved conflicts. In other cases, crises of life crash unexpectedly, driving normally peaceful people to the precipice of worry and fear.

Beth knew God loved her, but the uncertainties of her family's financial situation created constant pressure. Her husband, Frank, was immersed in trying to plant a church. Focused on the demands of ministry, he had thrust the responsibility of family management onto Beth. She was not prepared for the kinds of decisions she faced. Money was never abundant and, when the twins became ill, medical bills pushed their household budget over the edge. Weekly, she worried what might happen if even some of their stateside support wavered. Financial and emotional stress took a toll on her relationship with her husband, affected her discipline of the children, and caused her to resent attending the church that seemed unconcerned about their needs.

Faith does not erase the realities of financial difficulties or other problems. However, trust in a caring, capable Lord can empower Christians to endure when all efforts fail. Believers should realize God invites us to cast "all your care upon him; for he cares for you" (1 Peter 5:7).

Sensing God is far away. In some instances, personal sin can result in feelings of separation from God and the loss of salvation's joy (Psalm 51:11–12). In such cases, the problem is not mere stress, but sin, requiring repentance and cleansing. Stress-related issues, on the other hand, can cause believers to feel, without reason, that God has distanced Himself from them. Their prayers appear to go unanswered. Worship becomes formal and empty. Evangelism ceases because soul winning relies on a vital union between Christ and the witness.

Serious, consistent stress can cause missionaries to focus on circumstances and lose the awareness of God's presence. Without the constant companionship of the One Who called them, missionaries quickly lose heart. Ministers and their families have placed their lives on the line to follow Christ into difficult, distant places. They may feel isolated and alone. Few emotions are so desolate.

David, though king of Israel, felt that way at times. When his enemies gloated over his difficulties, David prayed, "This thou hast seen, O LORD: keep not silence: O Lord, be not far from me" (Psalm 35:22). In truth, God had never left David. His troubles pressed upon him so heavily that it seemed God was silent and far away. I've felt like that at times, and probably you have as well. We need to remember God is still near, and He speaks to us if we are willing to turn our eyes firmly on Him and listen.

Having difficulty worshipping, praying, or reading the Bible. People do not cease having devotional times of prayer and Bible reading because they merely fall out of the habit. In reality, both activities have one result—they bring us into the presence of God. Both sin and stress can transform one's perception of God from peace-giver to stressor. We tend to avoid sources of stress, so we avoid God when His presence convicts us of sin or if His calling results in an internal struggle to surrender to His will. We may avoid devotional time that constantly reminds us of something we want to do that we should not or something we should do and do not want. Consequently, we fail to pray or study Scripture because we are uncomfortable with God.

Spiritual weariness also creates disillusionment or discouragement that manifests itself in avoidance of spiritual devotions. While Paul urged believers not to become "weary in well doing," the reality is even the most sincere missionary becomes weary of spirit on occasion. Whether spiritual warfare with an unseen but ever-present enemy, or emotional stress from overextended compassion, the cause of weariness takes its toll. Part of the problem arises when missionary families try to accomplish the Lord's work on their own rather than within the yoke of Christ.

Ironically, the one place believers can find relief becomes the one place they do not go—to the Lord. He alone can give us strength for the task, determination for the fight, and peace for the spirit. Yet, unless we are willing to yield to Christ's direction, we will struggle with anything that creates an encounter with the Most High.

> *Unless we are willing to yield to Christ's direction, we will struggle with anything that creates an encounter with the Most High.*

Difficulty forgetting mistakes. Everyone makes mistakes. Stressed people have difficulty forgetting them. The nature of continual stress makes people susceptible to preoccupation with the past. Healthy persons exhibit a level of resilience that allows them to move past the past. However, when stress builds up over time, they can lose the ability to handle mistakes. Regrets accumulate, creating a constant burden of reliving blunders. The devil loves playing videos of our past across our minds, filling our hearts with a sense of remorse and failure.

Billie Jean displayed a growing sense of sadness. Even when she and her family were experiencing what should have been happy times, she never seemed to enjoy it fully. She took care of her family diligently and was active in her ministry setting, yet her melancholy continued. Finally agreeing to talk to a member care worker, she reluctantly shared about a series of judgment errors that occurred earlier in her life. Remorse and self-loathing had robbed her of contentment and joy. These feelings had lain dormant for years, but a series of stressful situations brought them again to the surface. Through spiritual counseling and the loving support of her husband, Billie Jean finally found forgiveness from her past mistakes and began moving forward with her life.

Persistent doubts. Shakespeare wrote: "Our doubts are traitors, and make us lose the good we oft might win, by fearing to attempt."[3] Questioning oneself, others, and even God may reveal more than lack of faith. Prolonged stress can make anyone second-guess everything and everyone. Lingering burdens weigh down one's spirit, wearying the sufferer. Resultant fatigue reduces resiliency when matters do not seem to improve.

We misunderstand the nature of doubt when we make it an intellectual exercise. Doubt is emotional in nature. Doubt and its first cousin, defeat, reflect someone who may be exhausted emotionally. Intellectual questions in such cases are rarely answered, for supposed solutions merely generate more queries. When afflicted by problems, the individual may ask why, as if understanding reasons for their dilemma would make them feel better.

Spiritual doubts may not be so much a crisis of faith as it could indicate an emotional reaction to ongoing pain. When unable to find relief from ongoing troubles, people may wonder about the nature of God and His providence. Like the disciples struggling in stormy seas, we approach a sleeping Savior and ask, "Don't You care?" (Mark 4:38). His answer then remains the same today; not only does He care, He is grieved that we would think He does not. He was able to calm the storm on the sea, and He is more than capable of calming the tempests in our hearts if we would trust Him and place our lives in His hands.

Excusing misdeeds. Severe stress can display itself in spiritual callousness and insensitivity to personal responsibility (Hebrews 3:15). One of the greatest dangers for ministers in any setting involves a sense of entitlement. Having surrendered much in the service of the Lord, we can fall prey to the belief that life (or God) owes us something. If we accept this premise, we excuse misdeeds, discounting them in light of our larger sacrifice.

Cindy did not really want to be on the field. She loved her husband and wanted to support his call to missions, so she found herself far away from her parents and friends. The stress of third-world culture, especially the lack of hygiene among the people where she lived, grew increasingly difficult. For comfort, she often went shopping in upscale stores on the other side of the city where she lived. At first, small items provided great pleasure, lifting her spirits for a time. However, increasingly she needed more expensive jewelry, clothes, and other merchandise to satisfy her craving. Lacking the income to support her habit, she began taking money from ministry funds. When confronted by the area supervisor, Cindy rationalized her sin by claiming she deserved extra money to compensate for everything she had given up. The consequences for herself and her family were serious and restitution took years.

Maintaining anger or bitterness. Nelson Mandela, jailed for twenty-seven years in apartheid South Africa, observed: "Resentment is like drinking poison and hoping your enemy dies." Scripture more pointedly warns that not handling anger quickly gives the devil "place" in our lives (Ephesians 4:27). Bitterness may reveal unmanaged stress because we are less open to forgiveness when we are under pressure, even if the source of stress has nothing to do with the source of the anger.

Tom was having numerous problems at home. Tension with his oldest son kept the stress level high. In an administrative meeting of his mission team, a colleague made a comment that hurt Tom deeply. Normally, Tom would have been able to shrug off the pain or at least work with the teammate to resolve the issue. Instead, the underlying stress at home found an outlet in Tom's anger toward his coworker. Only when a third party intervened did Tom realize what was happening and took action to resolve issues at work and at home.

When Peter confronted Simon, the magician who sought to purchase power, the apostle recognized the man had been poisoned by bitterness (Acts 8:23). Paul warned the Ephesians about the dangers of bitterness, wrath, anger, and malice (Ephesians 4:31). A believer who refuses to put away these sinful emotions and actions may experience spiritual and emotional stress.

Disregarding other people. People under stress tend to be self-focused. Even the most servant-hearted person becomes less able to invest in others when wrestling with personal pain. Members of the missionary's church, coworkers, even family may feel slighted when the stressed person does not respond to conversations, calls, or ministry needs. Spouses and children often receive the brunt of the strain and perceive they are being left out of a vital part of their loved one's life. The offenders do not necessarily intend to shun others; they merely concentrate on their own problems so much that they simply do not see the needs of people around them, even those closest to them.

Having too much or too little regard for material things. Christians should not be materialistic—having a value system based on things. At the same time, believers have stewardship over whatever part of creation God has placed into their hands. People under prolonged, unmanaged stress float in the direction of two extremes. Some personalities go into a buying or accumulation mode, using the gaining of material possessions as a kind of comfort food to elevate their mood. Unable to cope with whatever is causing the real problem, they find their emotions improving when amassing more "stuff."

On the other hand, many persons experiencing ongoing stress become almost oblivious of their belongings. Completely focused on their burden, they fail to take care of homes, vehicles, clothes, or other material matters. Clutter accumulates in their dwellings or offices, as they simply do not have the energy or concern to straighten up, dispose of trash, or take care of filing.

John's friends grew concerned when he became irregular at their weekly get-togethers and then dropped out altogether. They observed he seemed to be unconcerned about his personal appearance or needs of others around him. Visiting his home, they were alarmed to see the normally neat house dirty and disorderly. Sensing something deeper was happening, they intervened directly, discovered a deep hurt he had experienced, and began helping him cope. Once John came to grips with the underlying issue and renewed his relationship with Christ, he began to come around in all areas of his life and returned to productive interaction with family, friends, and ministry associates.

CHAPTER FIVE

Where Does Stress Come From?

Medical doctors use symptoms to trace origins of physical problems. Numbness in the hands or fingers can lead to a suspicion of carpel tunnel syndrome. Fever may indicate a bacterial infection or virus. Pain in the abdomen could indicate a number of issues related to internal organs. Symptoms tell the physician what tests need to be performed in order to identify the correct diagnosis. Only then can procedures or medication be prescribed to alleviate the condition.

Stress is different. A physical effect may have an emotional source. Emotional distress could emanate from a spiritual cause. People trying to manage stress in their lives or helping others dealing with stress-oriented problems must use observable evidence as warning signals. The flashing lights of stress' effects should provoke deeper analysis of the various areas of the sufferer's life to ascertain the source of the issue. Usually more than one problem emerges, requiring attention on several fronts at the same time.

Spiritual Causes

Sin

When God's people fall into sin, His Spirit is grieved (Ephesians 4:30). The sinner not only senses the Spirit's disquiet, his own spirit is disturbed. God designed us so that believers cannot sin and enjoy it. A believer who sins comes under conviction, which causes stress. Either the person repents and receives forgiveness or continues in sin with a hardening heart. At that point, God Himself becomes a source of stress because He reminds the person of the sin. Sinning Christians tend to avoid Bible study, prayer, and worship services because anything that brings them into the presence of God is disturbing.

Bob seemed especially touchy, Molly thought. He seemed unusually preoccupied and distant. Interactions with her and the children often devolved into bouts of anger that seemed to come out of nowhere. His ministry began to show signs of failure as his emotional imbalance bled over into the mission activities. Matters continued to grow worse until Bob reached a personal crisis that led him to seek help. He finally admitted to having become infatuated with a woman from a local tribe with which he had been working. His illicit attraction produced significant guilt feelings that manifested in his attacks on his family and coworkers. Only when repentance and confession produced a sense of forgiveness and relief did Bob return to being the man Molly had married.

Spiritual Warfare

No missionary can discount the reality of spiritual warfare surrounding the missionary enterprise. Herbert Kane warned: "Satan will not suffer his kingdom to be invaded or his authority challenged by the Christian missionary. Sooner or later the missionary will feel the full fury of his wrath."[1] Many mission workers have observed demonic manifestations in people they encounter, especially in locations where spiritism and idolatry run rampant.

Dr. Jerry Rankin, in his important work, *Spiritual Warfare*, recalls his first encounter with a demon-possessed person in Asia who, though having never learned our language, spoke in clear English, "Jesus Christ is not God." This occasion was not the last, or strangest, situation that Rankin had come across, but illustrates the reality of our enemy's power.[2] Rankin's book offers strong scriptural strategies for engaging spiritual battles.

Adults are not the only ones who come under the attack of Satan. Missionaries need to be on guard against Satan's attacks on their families. In his book, *Faith Under Fire*, Steven Lawson, declares: "The Christian life is a war. Not a playground for children, but a battleground for soldiers."[3]

Unfortunately, children get caught in this spiritual warfare, especially on the mission field. The devil targets teens and children without consideration or compassion. Satan can attack their minds through the secular and sensual stimuli of media. Their bodies may be afflicted with illness (not to say that all illness comes from the enemy). The same evil strategies adults encounter also affect children and teenagers.

Doubt

Doubt is not merely an intellectual problem; it has emotional and spiritual origins. Stressful circumstances challenge one's faith in the best of situations. Missionaries are not exempt from wrestling with doubt. Insufficient financial support, family illness, people groups who are resistant to the gospel, and legal problems are only a few attacks on personal belief. When God seems not to answer intense prayers, missionary families may struggle with their faith.

Arrested in a closed-culture nation, one worker spent a lengthy time in terrible prison conditions while his family was harassed as he helplessly waited and prayed. Recalling his feelings, he said, "My world went black. Why was God refusing to answer our prayers? Where was He now? . . . At that moment my belief systems collapsed. I felt God at least owed me an explanation." After being released, this worker commented that he returned to a deeper faith and understanding of the role of suffering in the Christian life.[4]

Doubt lingers in one's mind and heart like a stealthy enemy, denying its victim the peace and contentment that come from faith. People who harbor doubt often bear a distressed spirit as they wrestle with emotional challenges and questions of conviction.

Anger

While anger is an emotional symptom of stress, it can also be a spiritual cause of stress. Anger is a natural emotion, but often leads to bitterness and sin. Ephesians 4:26 indicates one can be angry but not sin. Consider the cause, expression, and results of anger. Human anger often results from the flesh or the self-nature (Ephesians 4:31; Galatians 5:19–21). While some people may excuse anger as righteous indignation, rarely does our wrath proceed from a defense of God's character. It more often comes from hurt feelings, wounded pride, or personal frustration.

Human anger rarely demonstrates the nature of God (James 1:19–20). Certainly, God's wrath is not sinful, but the wrath of man and the will of God are generally mutually exclusive. Human anger often leads to sins, including bitterness, hatred, revenge, judgment, and injury (Colossians 3:8). As a result, people need to learn how to control and cure anger.

Anger nearly always produces stress for everyone involved. Angry persons may express irritation as a result of stress afflicting their lives. The objects of their anger, as well as innocent bystanders, which often include family members, suffer the fallout of anger's verbal, behavioral, or emotional manifestations.

Correction

God loves us enough to introduce correction into our lives when we wander from His paths. "My son, despise not the chastening of the LORD; neither be weary of his correction: For whom the LORD loves he corrects; even as a father the son in whom he delights" (Proverbs 3:11–12). We dislike being corrected and often resist whatever God uses to produce repentance. Often, instead of responding positively to God's discipline, we try to overcome the means of chastisement. Dr. Charles Solomon once said, "God often fixes fixes to fix us. If we fix the fix God fixes to fix us before it fixes us, He will just fix another fix to fix us." His amusing statement has serious applications. Loving us, God will not relent as long as we remain in sin. The only real choice we have is to repent, confess, and return to our Father.

The process of correction, by its nature, causes stress. Internal disquiet of the spirit presses upon us, moving us away from sin's attraction. In this case, the stress may appear as distress but is actually eustress (good stress) because its purpose involves our restoration and renewal.

Certainly, we could address other examples of spiritual causes of stress. You may be experiencing one right now. The solution in each case remains the same—come to Jesus. Don't delay. Remember the admonitions of Hebrews: "Take heed, brethren, lest there be in any of you an evil heart of unbelief, in departing from the living God. But exhort one another daily, while it is called today; lest any of you be hardened through the deceitfulness of sin. For we are made partakers of Christ, if we hold the beginning of our confidence steadfast unto the end; While it is said, Today if you will hear his voice, harden not your hearts . . ." (Hebrews 3:12–15).

Physical Causes

Physical discipline, or the lack of it, affects not only how we respond to stress, but the way we treat our bodies can actually cause stress in other areas of life. Unlike the Gnostics of the early centuries who saw the body as evil and the spirit as good, Scripture teaches that we should care for our bodies as well as our souls. Paul prayed such for the people at Thessalonica: "And the very God of peace sanctify you wholly; and I pray God your whole spirit and soul and body be preserved blameless unto the coming of our Lord Jesus Christ" (1 Thessalonians 5:23).

To that end, the Bible encourages us to present our bodies a "living sacrifice, holy, acceptable unto God, which is your reasonable service" (Romans 12:1). Instead of surrendering to self-gratification, whether in sexual or gluttonous sin, we must discipline our bodies and bring them under subjection (1 Corinthians 9:27). Paul wanted to live in such a way that Christ would be magnified in his body, whether by life or death (Philippians 1:20). His prayer provides a worthy goal for each of us.

Some of the more obvious physical sources of stress include the following:

Weariness
Fatigue affects many areas of life. When we are tired, we make mistakes, use poor judgment, become angry more easily, and are more likely to compromise. Overwork, lack of sleep, long hours, and short nights tax the body and mind. When physical exertion goes beyond a certain point, exhaustion may set in. At that point, as someone has said, "The most spiritual thing we can do is take a nap." God gave His children the Sabbath as more than a one-day-a-week principle. He designed us to require regular rest so we can be refreshed and focus on Him. When we ignore God's pattern and

push ourselves beyond normal endurance, we become more susceptible to stress in all areas of life.

Sometimes weariness comes as we serve God. Instead of pursuing God's call in the power of His Spirit, we delude ourselves into thinking it is all up to us. With good intentions and zealous spirit, we nevertheless substitute physical and mental activity for the fruit of the Spirit. When the body and mind finally start to shut down, we falsely attribute our exhaustion to the Lord's work and blame our burnout on Him. Paul reminded the Galatians: "And let us not be weary in well doing: for in due season we shall reap, if we faint not" (Galatians 6:9).

Weariness may be more emotional and spiritual than physical. David wrote: "I am weary with my groaning; all the night I make my bed to swim; I water my couch with my tears" (Psalm 6:6). His personal grief not only denied him sleep but drained him of joy and vigor.

God wants to empower us for engaging His calling within the power of His spirit. We can trust His promise: "He gives power to the faint; and to them that have no might he increases strength" (Isaiah 40:29).

Poor Nutrition

People under stress tend to eat comfort food high in fat and cholesterol. Instead of preparing healthy meals, overly extended workers grab quick and available snacks or fast food that often are counterproductive to good health. Substituting healthy nourishment for junk food, they do not get the nutrition needed for well-being, causing stress reactions to have a negatively enhanced effect. In addition, fat and cholesterol can lead to coronary heart disease, stroke, and other physical problems. A high-fat diet also creates sluggishness. A high-fat content lunch may result in difficulty paying attention in afternoon meetings. Unhealthy people lack sufficient resistance to ward off viruses and other illnesses, adding to their stress.

While Christians are not subject to the dietary laws of the Old Testament, a diet guided by biblical principles will produce better health than the typical fare most people consume. We should take care of our bodies as the temple of the Holy Spirit. A healthy body enables believers to be more stress resilient.

Caffeine

Tea, coffee, soft drinks, and chocolate contain the Christian's "drug of choice"—caffeine. Caffeine is a stimulant that affects the central nervous system, increases blood pressure, and acts as a diuretic. Results of too much caffeine intake include restlessness, trembling, sleeplessness, and heart palpitations. It can also be addictive, making withdrawal difficult.[5]

Interestingly, many believers excuse their two or three cup-a-morning coffee habits as acceptable in order to provide needed energy for the day. Ironically, the caffeine addiction itself likely contributes to the morning sluggishness much like a hangover results from alcohol. Nervous jitters can be caused by too much coffee as much as through caffeine withdrawal.

Coffee is not the only source of the drug. Non-coffee users may revert to other sources to maintain their caffeine high. If you are a soft drink user, add up the number of ounces you consume in an average day. Take note of the amount of caffeine you ingest, along with the carbohydrate grams if the drink is not calorie-free. On the other hand, if you use diet drinks, do a study of the effects of aspartame before you start on that third diet drink of the day.

Chronic Pain

People who have not endured severe, chronic pain cannot understand the level of emotional stress sufferers experience. Pain from injury, illness, operations, and other causes feels the same—it hurts. Chronic pain not only leads some people to become addicted to pain-killing drugs, it affects their mental and emotional equilibrium.

Ongoing pain, of whatever intensity, nags at the mind and body. Demanding attention, pain causes lack of focus, often resulting in poor decisions. People with chronic pain may become less sensitive to other members of the family, friends, or coworkers. They tend to be more intolerant of whatever someone else does or says that adds to their discomfort.

Missionaries with muscular or skeletal problems, which most often are associated with chronic pain, may not have access to proper medical help, especially if complicated surgery is required. Faithful to the people they serve, workers may choose to endure the pain rather than leave the field for what may be a complicated operation and lengthy recuperation.

One of the most famous biblical examples of response to pain is Job. Although he stoically stayed steadfast through the initial losses, as time went by and his pain (physical and emotional) continued, he began to voice his complaint: "Therefore I will not refrain my mouth; I will speak in the anguish of my spirit; I will complain in the bitterness of my soul" (Job 7:11).

Paul experienced a "thorn in the flesh," which caused distress for several years. He prayed for relief, asking God to remove the problem. Most scholars believe Paul's issue was physical in nature. God declined to heal Paul, reminding the apostle that His strength was made perfect in Paul's weakness (2 Corinthians 12:9). Most of us would struggle with such a response. We need healing, and we know God remains the Great Physician, able to heal. Accepting His answer, especially when it means continuing pain, challenges our faith. It can make us or break us at the point not only of believing God, but trusting that even pain can be used by Him for our good (Romans 8:28).

Illness and Injury

Sickness and injuries create stress. In addition to the obvious physical implications, they add to emotional distress as well. They add to emotional distress as well. Missionaries may not have available or competent health care, adding to their stress.

Family members find it difficult to watch loved ones live through ongoing pain. Especially when the patient is a child or teenager, parents experience pain alongside their children. They want to "make it better." Unfortunately, these kinds of problems cannot be healed simply with a mother's kiss.

One minister's family suffered over two years of mental anguish as their child was treated for leukemia. The youngster endured scores of difficult treatments. He experienced remission for a while, but continued to risk infection and other setbacks. He and his family suffered mental and emotional pain as well. The toll on everyone was tremendous. Only through the grace of God were they able to endure.

Emotional Causes

Regrets

Too many people live in the "if only's" of life. Focusing on the past, they cannot escape what might have been. Former sins and mistakes haunt their present and endanger their future. Relationships suffer when they drag the baggage of remorse wherever they go. Regrets include acts they wish they had not done as well as opportunities missed along the way. They constantly obsess over small and large decisions that ended poorly. Just when they think they have left the past in the rearview mirror, the devil, the accuser of the brethren, beats them over the head with renewed regret.

God does not want His children living in defeat. Paul struggled with his realities, yet found victory through Jesus Christ (Romans 7:19–25). God desires to set our sin as far from us as the east from the west (Psalm 103:12). Christ's blood cleanses the repentant believer from all sin (1 John 1:9). Through Him, we can forget what is behind and reach out to whatever God has before us (Philippians 3:13–14).

When we neglect such a great salvation and try to accomplish the Christian life within our own abilities, we inevitably fall short. The flesh is not designed for victorious Christian living. Without Christ's Spirit filling our hearts with hope for the future, we will remain bound by chains of the past like Marley's ghost in Dickens' *A Christmas Carol*.

Fear

Fear generally relates to some present consequence, circumstance, or person. Faith's opposite, fear can paralyze people, preventing them from making positive decisions that influence their future. Some people fear facing the consequences of past errors. Others see circumstances of life as turning out to be the worst outcome possible.

Paul reminded Timothy that "God has not given us the spirit of fear; but of power, and of love, and of a sound mind" (2 Timothy 1:7). The only fear we ought to have is the reverential fear of the Lord (Deuteronomy 17:19; Psalm 110:10). To the contrary, as we serve the Lord, we can be strong and courageous, rebuking fear because God is faithful. As Moses told Joshua, "Be strong and of a good courage, fear not, nor be afraid of them:

for the LORD thy God, he it is that doth go with thee; he will not fail thee, nor forsake thee (Deuteronomy 31:6).

The great lessons of the Old Testament demonstrate Israel mainly found itself in trouble when they feared the wrong thing. Fearing their enemies instead of God, they made poor choices. Abraham feared for his life, so he lied about his relationship with Sarah to protect himself (Genesis 12, 20). Aaron compromised the entire nation when he made a golden idol out of fear of the people (Exodus 32). Israel wandered forty years in the wilderness instead of enjoying God's Promised Land because most of their advance team feared the Canaanite forces (Numbers 14:1–5; Deuteronomy 1:26–28).

The New Testament also points out the failure of fear. Nicodemus came to Jesus at night for fear of his peers (John 3). Joseph of Arimethaea was a secret disciple until the crucifixion forced him to courageous deeds (John 19). The disciples were afraid of a storm (Matthew 8:26), the appearance of Jesus upon the water (Mark 6:50), and the arrival of armed guards to arrest Jesus (Matthew 26:56). Peter denied knowing Jesus out of fear (John 18). Pilate, although desiring to release Jesus, turned Him over to be crucified out of fear (John 19). Hebrews describes people who were in bondage because of fear of death (Hebrews 2:15). Stress constantly accompanies the fearful.

We ought to respond to frightening circumstances by boldly saying, "The Lord is my helper, and I will not fear what man shall do unto me (Hebrews 13:6). Let us not yield timidly and miss God's glorious provision. As Shakespeare put it, "Cowards die many times before their deaths; the valiant never taste of death but once."[6]

Worry

Scripture constantly urges believers not to be anxious, worried, or fearful of the future. People who lack a virile faith find themselves obsessed by what *might* happen. Instead of believing that God is and that He is a rewarder of those who diligently seek Him (Hebrews 11:6), they worry over worst-case possibilities. Worry is the worm in the juiciest apple, the rot in the finest wood, and the thief of joy and happiness in a believer's life.

Paul urged the Christians at Philippi to be worried about nothing but instead to bring their requests to God through prayer and thanks-filled supplication. Such an act of faith produces the peace of God beyond our understanding, which will guard our hearts and minds through Christ (Philippians 4:6-7).

Mental Causes

Computer programmers have a common saying: "Garbage in, garbage out," meaning whatever you put into the computer is what you get out. Similarly, what goes into one's mind affects one's outlook. Paul urged the Philippian Christians to think on those things that are true, honest, just, pure, lovely, of good reputation, virtuous, and praiseworthy (Philippians 4:8). He told the Romans to be transformed by the renewing of their minds (Romans 12:2). Conversely, we can fill our minds with unhealthy thoughts through the ever-present channels of worldly communication.

The Desensitizing Effect of Secular Media

Christians rarely make a plunge into sin in one dramatic dive. Instead, they gradually become desensitized to sin by improperly using various media controlled by people who dislike or disregard moral values. Watching television shows or movies that are violent, dark, sexual, profane, or filled with secular worldviews will gradually affect any family.

Reading material that is not edifying can fashion a fleshly mindset. Believers should not only avoid those items containing pornographic or otherwise inappropriate content, but also stay away from materialism. Magazines focusing on materialism, glamor, and financial success lure readers away from what is edifying and good.

Music and music videos also have a powerful impact, especially on teens. Someone asked the head of a major television network that focuses on music videos about the influence his company had on teenagers. He replied that his network does not just influence teens. He is reported to have said: "We own them."

In some areas, both in the United States and overseas, the nuclear family tended to be fairly cohesive and culturally consistent from generation to generation. Geographical limitations prevented cable television from reaching many of the homes. The satellite dish opened Pandora's Box of sensuality for teens and adults alike, creating damaging input that affected church planters' families as much as any other home. The Internet multiplied the problem exponentially.

Media in international settings can often be even more harmful than that in the United States. In Europe and other primarily secular venues, the danger may not only be in openly sexual content, but also in a worldview that denies biblical truth, the existence of God, creation, and other foundational beliefs. Exposure through television, secular education, and peer pressure can strongly impact teens and children whose impressionable minds are more open to such influences.

Sometimes, the cultural boredom of missionary venues becomes the rationale for using materials that harm instead of edify. Without ready access to spiritually healthy media, family members may gravitate to what is available rather than what is good and godly.

The Peril of the Internet

Internet pornography is a common source of sensual perversion and a growing danger among ministers' families. Many men and women have become addicted to sexual content over the Internet. One minister called his missions leader asking for help with his marriage after his wife found him watching pornography on his home computer. Another minister lost his position when his secretary walked into his office unannounced, only to find him ogling sexual content on his office computer. What was once required a risky trip to the wrong side of the tracks is now available at the click of a button in the privacy of one's home or office. The advent of smartphones with instant Internet access adds a portable dimension to the temptation.

More dangerous are the virtual vamps who troll cyberspace seeking young minds to pervert.

Unsupervised Internet access by teens and children endangers their developing minds. Curious by nature, fueled by newly discovered hormones, teens may experiment with sites discovered accidentally in otherwise innocent searches for valid information. Spamware pop-ups also lurk behind legitimate websites, waiting for naïve victims. Proverbs warns against the idle mind enticed by a seducing temptress. More dangerous are the virtual vamps who troll cyberspace seeking young minds to pervert.

In some extreme situations, lonely missionary spouses may turn to virtual relationships through Internet chat rooms. A wife may become involved with a man through chat room conversations. Perhaps the husband was often away and did not give her the attention she needed when he was home. She might begin chatting just to find companionship, someone to talk with. The chat partner will tell her what she wants to hear, and she may become infatuated with him. She could begin to fantasize about what life would be with her chat partner. Will the matter be discovered and godly counsel help save the marriage, or will the virtual relationship dissolve the real one?

The Internet, like any technology, can provide many positive benefits from access to study materials to communication with family back home. On the other hand, it can also become the source of mental infections that eat away at moral and spiritual foundations.

Entertaining Wicked Thoughts

Prior to the great Flood, God "saw that the wickedness of man was great in the earth, and that every imagination of the thoughts of his heart was only evil continually" (Genesis 6:5). The problem of wicked imaginations and evil thoughts did not end with the deluge. Scripture describes people as having "despiteful minds" (Ezekiel 36:5), "hardened minds" (Daniel 5:20), "doubtful minds" (Luke 12:29), "evil (poisoned) minds" (Acts 14:2), "darkened minds" (Romans 1:21), "reprobate minds" (Romans 1:28), "carnal minds" (Romans 8:6), "blinded minds" (2 Corinthians 3:14), "hostile minds" (Colossians 1:21), and "defiled minds" (Titus 1:15).

Deceitful persons may try to conceal foul intent by doing what appears to be good, but even sacrificial worship is polluted when the heart is evil. Proverbs warns: "The sacrifice of the wicked is abomination: how much more, when he brings it with a wicked mind?" (Proverbs 21:27).

Evil thoughts pour in through media, a corrupt world, and ungodly acquaintances, but the worst imaginations may originate from our own fleshly desires. A worker whose family struggles with having basic needs may entertain jealous thoughts toward a coworker who seems to have more. Jealousy can degenerate into bitterness and even hatred. A missionary who is having marital difficulties may let his mind begin to dwell on an attractive woman. Mental wanderings can grow into lustful plans and disastrous actions. Jesus warned about the link between one's thought life and sinful deeds (Matthew 5:28).

God does not want us to be slaves to fleshly thoughts. He gives us the power through His Spirit and His Word to be transformed by the renewing of our minds (Romans 12:2). Paul advised the Ephesian Christians to "put off concerning the former conversation the old man, which is corrupt according to the deceitful lusts; And be renewed in the spirit of your mind" (Ephesians 4:22–23).

Believers would benefit by daily praying along with David: "Search me, O God, and know my heart: try me, and know my thoughts: And see if there be any wicked way in me, and lead me in the way everlasting" (Psalm 139:23–24). God gives us the spiritual ability to cast down evil imaginations and bring every thought into captivity (2 Corinthians 10:3–5). However, if we yield to the natural, fleshly instincts under the stress of life, our thoughts will take us captive instead.

Self-Centered Thinking

Missionaries are generally "others oriented" in their mindset. However, even God's choicest workers can fall prey to focusing on themselves. In some cases, success becomes a snare and we may begin to think how good we are. Even Jesus' disciples allowed their experiences with Jesus to delude them into thinking they all were great; the only question was who was the greatest! "Jesus, perceiving the thought of their heart, took a child, and set him by him, And said unto them, Whosoever shall receive this child in my name receives me: and whosoever shall receive me receives him that sent me: for he that is least among you all, the same shall be great" (Luke 9:47–48).

We might think that one object lesson from the Lord would be enough. However, the disciples continued to suffer from self-centered thinking. Even the Sons of Thunder, James and John, sought to claim special privilege in Christ's kingdom. Amidst the ensuing dispute with the other disciples, Jesus intervened, teaching them, "whosoever will be great among you, shall be your minister: And whosoever of you will be the chief, shall be servant of all" (Mark 10:43–44).

At the Last Supper, Jesus had just told the disciples that His betrayer was at the table with them. While they first wondered about the culprit's identity, they quickly digressed into an argument over which one of them would be the greatest, prompting Jesus to rebuke them again (Luke 22:23–26).

Self-centered thinking makes life all about us rather than God. We come to believe that life, even God, owes us something. We may even claim success in ministry as if it were our doing rather than the work of God. Pride, jealousy, bitterness, envy—nearly every sinful thought we entertain can be traced to self-centered thinking.

Developmental Issues

Children

Doctors increasingly are treating children for the effects of stress. One study observed that by six years of age, many children have developed patterns of emotional and mental behavior that lead to severe hypertension.[7] The dramatic changes of the mission field can affect children more dramatically than teens or adults, especially if parents neglect nurturing their children in order to tend to the vast needs of the indigenous people.

On the other hand, children whose parents provide a strong nurturing environment often share the family's commitment for the people they serve. Prayer requests from children on the mission field demonstrate the kinds of issues they face and the manner in which they respond. Some are concerned for grandparents stateside who have physical or other problems. Many pray that they might find friends in their new towns, often expressing that their friends might come to believe in Jesus.

Yet, even the ability to focus on the spiritual needs of people in their mission field does not immunize children from the effects of stress. God blesses their childlike faith and innocent love. They are strengthened as they receive His grace to deal with the pressures of the field. Still, even their desires for the salvation of their people groups can be a type of stress in itself. Their parents need to recognize levels of stress children are experiencing and give special attention to helping them.

Teens

While all teenagers experience stress, girls especially have difficulties related to gender and developmental stage. Dr. Roni Cohen-

Sandler notes: "Pressure comes from everyone—parents, teachers, media, friends, boyfriends, coaches." Unfortunately, teenage girls tend to avoid acknowledging their stressors because of fear of repercussions, reluctance to raise parental anxiety, low self-confidence worsened by admitting flaws, and comparing themselves to unrealistic ideals.[8]

Girls are also twice as likely as boys to develop depression. Unfortunately, their problems are often dismissed as a "growing phase or hormonal change," leaving them without support when they need it the most.[9]

Male teens not only contend with physical and hormonal changes, but boys on the mission field often feel they have to be "the man of the family" when Dad travels to remote locations. Young men wrestle with internal and external pressures that suppress their openness, making it unmanly to share intense emotions or confusing thoughts. Facing choices regarding career and dating or marriage, males may experience anger when their location in a foreign culture restricts their options.

Teenagers in missionary families, however, are often very strong in their commitment to the people their family serves. Their love for their national friends helps them overcome the kinds of stress that teens typically experience back home.

Missionary parents can help by treating them as children and teens, not just missionary kids (MKs), while recognizing the unique stresses in their lives. Taking time to listen to each one and respond to their fears, anxieties, and dreams goes a long way to helping MKs realize they have loving, supportive parents who deeply care about them.

Middle Age

They are called the Sandwich Generation. People in midlife often have aging parents, grandchildren, and sometimes still have teens at home. Persons in their 40s and 50s find it difficult to balance family demands in the relatively normal culture of their homeland. On the mission field, the challenges of dealing with extended family needs can overwhelm the strongest of committed missionaries.

As their parents grow older and need exceptional care, missionaries who lack siblings or other family face the dilemma of leaving the field or placing their parents in nursing homes or other facilities. Whichever choice they make, missionaries may suffer guilt. If they go home to care for their parents, they regret leaving unreached people behind on the field. If they stay, they worry about their parents being in an institution without family to visit and care for them.

A different type of pressure relates to middle-aged missionaries whose adult children have established themselves back in the homeland. They have married and have children, but the kinds of interactions between the children and their grandparents are limited to phone or Skype contacts due to the distance. Grandparenting missionaries can provide a strong witness for Christ as they relate to their grandchildren through whatever means is available while maintaining enthusiasm for their work on the field. The grandchildren may even be inspired to follow in their grandparents' missionary footsteps when they grow up. Still, the pangs of longing to hold and be present for their grandchildren produce significant levels of stress on the grandparents.

Missionaries also experience normal midlife crises related to hormonal changes, especially in women. Menopause produces physical and emotional challenges as women reach middle age. Some missionaries work in places where competent medical help may not be readily available. In addition, certain cultures have mores that make dealing with female problems especially difficult. Husbands of women experiencing menopause need knowledge and understanding to make this change of life manageable for their wives. Nevertheless, this experience will involve significant stress on both.

Men also experience midlife crises. Some men face the death of their dreams when life goals appear unreachable. Perhaps they came to the mission setting expecting to lead large numbers of people to Christ or start a church-planting movement, only to experience fruitless rejection after ministering for years with only a few converts. Other men have career goals that might include advancement within the mission agency but fail to achieve those aspirations.

Men also become especially vulnerable to various temptations at this age, including sexual, financial, and other types of challenges. One missionary became involved with a local woman and subsequently left his wife and lost his ministry. Unfortunately, this story is not isolated or unique. Some men may blame their wives or offer other excuses for immoral behavior, but the reality is that missionaries are not exempt from sexual temptation. The developmental issues of middle age make some men more vulnerable during this stage of life.

Older Missionaries

Aging missionaries encounter health needs, often in locations that lack medical care. Distance may prevent family members from helping. Some agencies provide on-the-field support systems that include not only medical aid but physical, spiritual, and emotional help. Missionaries who rely on deputation for their financial support may lack the resources necessary to deal with medical problems and remain on the field.

Older missionaries may not be able to endure some of the hardships required in going to distant locations where many unreached people groups live. Workers who have been active all their lives become frustrated and stressed by their inability to maintain previous levels of ministry.

Missionaries who have given their lives to a people group on the mission field may experience stress when facing retirement. They do not want to leave people who have become part of their families. In many ways, the place where they have served has become more like home than the towns where they grew up. Their friends are on the field, not back in the States. By this stage of life, these missionaries have acclimated to the local culture so much that returning to their homeland is almost like going to a foreign country. The thought of readjustment can be very stressful.

Returning, many missionaries face the problem of housing. Missionaries often live in mission agency housing or rental properties. They lack a financial foundation of home equity for retirement. Also, missionaries by nature are giving people. Like Lottie Moon who starved herself to give food to the Chinese children around her, many missionaries sacrifice whatever small stipend they receive to minister to the people of their mission field. Even agency-sponsored missionaries often lack ministry funds, forcing them to use personal income to pay for Bibles, evangelistic tools, food for hungry people, or other needs. Many missionaries come to the end of their ministries without sufficient savings to provide a home or retirement income. Such problems add significant stress to an already pressure-filled situation.

Mission-Specific Stressors

In addition to the normal origins of stressors experienced by average people, missionaries have situational stress unique to their ministries. Dr. Dorothy Gish of Messiah College observed sources of stress among missionary families: [10]

1. Communicating across language and cultural barriers
2. Time and effort raising and keeping financial support
3. Amount of work with multiple priorities
4. Need for pastoral care and a confident
5. Making decisions that affect others' lives
6. Extended family concerns
7. Lack of time for family and self

Consider how each of the following issues affects the missionary family:

1. *Cross-Cultural Communication and Conflict*

Most mission agencies invest substantial time and effort preparing workers for the challenges of cross-cultural experiences. Yet, nothing short of actual experience can ready missionary families for the many varieties of cultural stress. Spending a year in language school helps missionaries and their children communicate, but only immersion into the culture within a foreign land can produce understanding. Subtle cultural triggers may remain unknown until an unintentional offense launches the missionary or, worse, his wife and children into a conflict.

2. *Fundraising*

Given the immense needs in most mission fields, no worker or mission agency ever has enough money for all the opportunities and needs. Even missionaries associated with strong mission groups may have sufficient personal income but lack money for ministry expenses. For those workers dependent on deputation, the constant consciousness of sources of support can pull their attention from the field, creating a focus and fear regarding resources. Instead of being able to concentrate on the work at hand, many missionaries invest substantial time and energy in the process of finding and maintaining support.

3. *Multiple Priorities*

Most ministers begin to wonder if they are like the juggler trying to keep several balls in the air at the same time. Whether in a stateside ministry or an international venue, missionaries may struggle with multiple, often conflicting, priorities. The normal responsibilities of raising a family, providing education, and nurturing godly missionary kids run parallel with the needs for counseling, witnessing, organizing, committee meetings, report writing, governmental demands, and a hundred other issues.

Most MKs understand the nature of their parents' work and support, even help, in the various aspects of the ministry. At the same time, they are children. They want their parents' attention, care, and counsel. They need to have fun and enjoy family and friends like any other children or teenagers. Adults can easily become conflicted when one priority requires another to go unmet, sometimes causing hurt feelings or regrets.

4. *Personal Support and Counsel*

Missionaries and their families are not immune to personal crises. When family or marriage conflicts erupt, the average stateside family can turn to their pastors for counsel and encouragement. If nothing else, having someone to listen and share experiences provides much-needed assistance. On the mission field, however, missionaries may be separated from such resources by many miles. The availability of communication via satellite phones or Internet cannot substitute for the presence of another human being.

Increasingly, mission agencies make a priority of having Member Care personnel available for crises. Regular visits, supplemented by crises interventions, give some measure of support. In many cases, however, the problems are prevalent and pervasive. Not having a close confidante results in missionaries fending for themselves emotionally as well as physically.

5. *Affecting Others' Lives*

Missionaries are leaders by nature. Leaders constantly make decisions that affect not only themselves and their families but the people with whom they work. Decisions include allocation of financial and physical resources, strategic application of ministry programs, leadership choices, and time management. Most of those decisions produce wonderful results and bless everyone involved. Sometimes, leaders must make difficult choices that negatively affect others. Having to discipline an errant believer or admonish another worker must be done, but generally causes stress for the leader as well as the person being corrected. Making changes in leadership against the wishes of persons involved in an organization also falls into the category of stressful, but necessary. Most of all, when adult missionaries have to make tough choices that affect their families, they endure personal pressure and stress.

6. *The Family Back Home*

In another section, we addressed the Sandwich Generation that must manage aging parents back home along with teenagers and young adult children. Here, the concern goes beyond care for one's parents. Being away from the extended family means being absent from birthdays, holidays, and those special occasions that bring families together. Brothers and sisters may not understand why their missionary relatives chose to live so far away from them. MKs miss the joy of growing up with cousins, uncles, aunts, and grandparents. Especially when extended family members go through crises, missionary families grieve over not being at hand to help. While they can pray, call, and care, they can't be present to hold a hand, hug a neck, weep together, or laugh together. Regret and tension over family issues can strain even the most dedicated missionary families.

7. *Personal Attention*

With so many important demands on their time, missionaries often feel conflicted when they take time for themselves or their families. After all, eternal destines are being decided through their daily ministry. Workers may feel guilty if they take time to rest or set aside ministry concerns to relax. While some missionaries take advantage of their far-flung locations to visit interesting places and have fun with their families, others feel stressed by having to take vacations or furloughs. Many workers feel driven to stay at the work without consideration for their own or their family's needs for rest and recuperation.

Missionaries need to realize they are more effective by gaining physical, emotional, mental, and spiritual refreshment. Sometimes putting a little distance between oneself and the work actually helps the ministry by gaining new perspective and reengaging with renewed vigor.

Environmental Causes

Noise

Missionaries, like other families, wage a constant battle with stress caused by noise and clutter. These two conditions share a similar condition: overstimulation of the senses. Children are naturally noisy. They strive for attention by crying as infants, talking loudly as children, and blasting the home with music as teenagers (although the advent of earbuds helps). Adults may handle arguments between siblings or shouting by a single child or teen for a while, but before long, even the most patient parents can lose their tempers when the noise reaches a certain level. Particularly if one or both parents already have had a long, stressful day, an evening with crying babies, arguing teens, or friction with each other, it can push them over the emotional cliff.

Noise can invade through the general environment. Whether its music or television at home, traffic around the house, or even animals around the house, noise forces its way into the most placid of homes. Our daughter's family lived for a while in suburban Brisbane, Australia, across the street from an entryway to the forest. They never quite got used to the incredibly loud frogs at night and the noisy birds in the early morning.

Finding a moment of quiet, much less quiet contemplation, can be difficult in many missionary settings. They may have to enforce a quiet time each evening when everyone goes to their bedrooms to read, pray, or just enjoy the peacefulness of silence. In some cases, quarters are cramped and several children have to share rooms. Private space may be their beds. Some locations are situated near parks, woods, or cultural venues such as art galleries or museums where a reasonable quiet environment can be expected.

However and wherever they find it, mission families need some regular measure of relief from the constant invasion of noise. Each family member needs to cultivate quietness or risk being overwhelmed by the stress of surround sound.

Clutter

While noise produces aural stimulation, clutter creates visual stimulation. Time management specialists advise people to work in a clutter-free environment because of the mental distractions clutter produces. One does not have to be a neat freak to be stressed by a messy home or office. Having a home or work area filled with stuff creates multiple visual disruptions, resulting in a constant level of stress, much like the way a constant hum or hammering affects the auditory sense.

A seemingly sensible solution would be to clean out the clutter, organize the home, and maintain order. Such a plan sounds easy to people accustomed to tidy environments. However, many people, especially those with overwhelmingly busy schedules, develop higher tolerances for disorder, making it difficult for them to keep up with normal organization and environmental maintenance. They need help from others in the family to recognize the problem and keep the home or workplace as clutter-free as possible.

Travel/Traffic

Many missionaries come from churches in the open country, small towns, or modest cities in the United States. Traffic rarely becomes a source of stress and the only major delays tend to be during harvest season when the occasional tractor or combine lumbers down the highway. On the mission field, travel can produce significant stress in cities like New York, Chicago, Los Angeles, Moscow, Calcutta, or Berlin. The sheer press of people and vehicles can be overwhelming to someone from Yazoo City, Mississippi.

A common missionary saying is "Your car is only as fast as the ox cart in front of you." In many places, you cannot travel quickly. Roads, particularly in rural areas of second- and third-world countries, present obstacle courses of potholes and pedestrians. Geography in mountainous locations turn speedometers useless as travel is measured in hours rather than miles as one meanders back and forth through countless hairpin turns over multiple mountain ranges.

Pollution fills the streets of many cities where emissions controls are nonexistent and older vehicles, particularly large buses and trucks, emit clouds of black smoke as oil burns freely in worn-out motors. Beggars inundate drivers stopped by intersections or inevitably slow traffic.

Stress can build up quickly, especially if a crisis requires you to get somewhere quickly and the kids are crying in the backseat. Dislike of travel-related stress can press workers to cocoon themselves in missionary housing, venturing out only when absolutely necessary. When forced to travel, they may arrive at ministry venues without the emotional or spiritual frame of mind conducive to effective service.

Light and Darkness

Missionaries living above and below certain latitudes experience much longer days during the summer and extremely long nights during the winter. Coping with daylight from 4:30 a.m. to midnight can create problems sleeping, creating biological challenges and resulting in stress. Similarly, long periods of darkness have similar biological effects that can become depressive over an extended time.

Missionaries quickly learn coping skills from local people. Sunlamps help in places with extended darkness. When daylight extends past bedtime, hanging blackout curtains helps, but nothing ever quite overcomes the constant battle with light.

Uncleanness

Some locations have problems with sanitation and general uncleanness. In many third-world countries, basic sewage systems are nonexistent. New missionaries travelling in rural areas of India, the Philippines, Africa, and other countries may be shocked to see local children and adults alike urinating or defecating alongside the road. Homes suffer a permanent patina of dust due to having windows open to circulate air in the absence of air conditioning. In such places, concepts of cleanliness and personal hygiene are luxuries.

Many of these countries lack readily available clean water. In one trip to Port-de-Paix, Haiti, our missions group went three days before a delivery truck arrived with bottled water. Prior to the truck's arrival, the local pastor treated a large container of water with purifiers in case we ran out of drinking water. Most local people cannot afford bottled water. Their dependence on whatever local water source is available often creates a major problem not only of maintaining hygiene, but of contracting parasites and infectious diseases.

Missionaries employ purification systems and other means to help provide a clean environment for their families. However, even when their homes are relatively clean, missionary families live in constant interaction with other people, houses, businesses, churches, and public places that lack basic cleanliness.

Ministry also breeds unexpected health problems. A worker sent home a photo of his wife sitting on the floor with a national woman kneeling behind her. The national was doing a humble task of servanthood by picking lice out of the worker's long hair. She had contracted the pest by inviting homeless children into her house for food and Bible stories. Willing to expose oneself to unclean conditions to minister to needy children is typical of missionaries in many parts of the world.

A constant environment of uncleanliness creates stress on missionaries accustomed to standards of the West, where "cleanliness is next to godliness."

Danger

Believers are not safe anywhere. Whether threatened by a gunman forcing his way into an American church service or a hostile crowd approaching Asian churches with torches, Christians face danger everywhere they serve Jesus. Jesus warned His followers that people would hate them and persecute them because of Him (John 15:18–20). In an age that has seen more martyrs than any other period of history, modern missionaries realize they and their families are utterly dependent on the Lord for protection.

Most mission agencies try to prepare workers for dangerous contingencies, especially if they are serving in hazardous locations. However, the reality of peril produces a constant undercurrent of stress. Missionaries may come to peace at the thought of risking their lives for Christ, but knowing their families are also vulnerable never quite leaves their minds. Effective ministry in such circumstances requires us to give ourselves by faith into the hands of a faithful God, depending on Him for protection and provision.

The Press of the People

Many cultures do not value personal space the same way as people in Western societies. The sheer mass of people living in congested conditions causes nationals to become accustomed to having other people in close proximity. On a five-hour van ride through northwest Haiti, I recognized slight feelings of claustrophobia as fifteen people and three chickens crowded into a vehicle meant for eight passengers. Natural concern about health may compound discomfort caused by numbers of people pressing around one's person. The nature of public transportation, marketplaces, and tourist locations can be distressing to someone not accustomed to multitudes of people nearby.

Compassion

On her first mission trip to Moscow, my wife encountered street beggars for the first time. Her heart was broken by old women and young children sitting in the dirt and crying out for help. Many of the babushkas (grandmothers) of post-Soviet Russia had lost government pensions to restructuring and had lost husbands to alcoholism and suicide, leaving them without means for supporting themselves other than begging.

In India, I witnessed women begging at nearly every intersection of major cities. Some were victims of professional begging syndicates that enslaved women, often mutilating their faces or even cutting off one or both hands to make them more pitiable. A few women held infants. Some babies had been rented from their parents to lend heart-moving motivation to the beggars' pleas for help.

Beyond beggars, most mission fields, particularly urban areas, contain millions of the extreme poor. Many families live on the streets, under trees and bridges, or in shacks made of cast-off pieces of wood or cardboard. In Brazil, I was overwhelmed by thousands of people living in the barrios without basic food, clothing, housing, or hope. The thought arrested my mind: *My grandfather's pigs have better food and housing than these people.*

On a mission trip to Mexico, our group stayed in pop-up tents and RVs, camping out on the side of a mountain near a lone house where a family with several children lived. The youth had purchased hot dogs at a nearby store on the way to the mountain site. They did not eat the meal, disliking the taste of soy-based food. When they threw the cold wieners out into the dirt, they were amazed to witness the local children fighting the family dogs to retrieve the soiled food. Seeing extreme poverty firsthand transformed these middle-class, naïve kids, while, at the same time, seizing their hearts with an unease—a good kind of stress that would change their lives.

Missionaries are compassionate by nature. Seeing hurting people pains them. They experience stress as they encounter masses of people with enormous needs.

Financial Stress

Financial challenges not only include basic salary, housing, insurance, and retirement provisions. Missionaries must also deal with logistical support regarding travel, visas, child care, medical needs, training, programs, and ministries. In working with missionaries on six continents, I have never found anyone who did not encounter significant challenges regarding lack of financial resources. At the same time, I never met a single missionary who complained or became bitter over lack of funds. My personal experience does not mean that no problem exists; rather it testifies to missionaries' deep commitment to Christ and to the people of their mission fields. They trusted God in going to the field, and they trust God as they minister on the field. Still, the reality of insufficient funding provides constant stress on most missionary families.

Missionaries generally must demonstrate financial stability before going to the mission field. As time goes by, the manner of financial support creates varying levels of stress. Missionaries supported by denominational agencies generally are more secure than workers who depend on supporters. However, even strong agencies are unable to keep up with the needs of a worldwide field with increasingly open doors of opportunity, coupled with growing numbers of families responding to God's call to missions.

In some situations, missionaries are placed on the field with personal support but lack funds for effective ministry tools. As mentioned previously, many missionaries end up drawing from personal resources to provide for ministry needs. When these missionaries visit the States or read about churches back home, they often witness vast sums spent by churches on expensive building programs or other projects. One might understand their frustration in viewing what they consider extravagances among relatively churched populations in comparison to the huge needs they face on an unreached field and limited resources for ministry.

Missionaries who rely on deputation not only must raise funds for their personal and ministry support, but they have to maintain their income while separated from their donors. One source asserts that 43 percent of such missionaries never complete deputation.[11] Inevitably, contributors decrease or discontinue funding. Returning home to raise new supporters not only takes time away from ministry, it also places additional stress on missionary families who worry if they can return to their calling.

Missionaries are faith-based creatures by nature. They trust God's call and continue to trust His care. They believe Jesus who told His followers not to be anxious about the temporal needs of life since their heavenly Father knows they have these needs and loves to provide for them (Matthew 6:25–34). Such faith does not mean missionaries should not work hard and use financial prudence. Jesus' admonition in verse 34 does not mean believers can presume on God's providence and be irresponsible or careless. ("Take therefore no thought for the morrow: for the morrow shall take thought for the things of itself. Sufficient unto the day is the evil thereof.") Rather, the primary answer to financial stress is to forsake fear of the future and focus first on God's kingdom and His righteousness, believing God will provide. "But seek ye first the kingdom of God, and his righteousness; and all these things shall be added unto you" (Matthew 6:33).

Cross-Cultural Stress

One does not have to travel overseas to experience cross-cultural challenges. Thousands of missionaries live in the United States, but work in areas foreign to the culture in which they were raised. Southern families face quite an adjustment when serving in pioneer fields where the weather, culture, accents, food, and even housing may be vastly different. Similarly, a suburban Californian faces culture shock when ministering in the rural South.

Herbert Kane observes that culture shock occurs in stages. The first happens on arrival at the field. Depending on the degrees of difference from one's home culture, the shock may be mild or severe. In many third-world locations, crises can begin immediately on deplaning. The lack of cleanliness, scores of people grabbing for your baggage, differences in language, money, customs, legalities, and climate are just a few of the initial adjustments.[12]

The excitement of a challenge motivates many new missionaries. The second stage begins when the newness wears off while trying to learn a new language, adapt to a new culture, begin ministry among people who may not be receptive to foreigners, handle illness and other crises, and enter the season after season of missions work. Kane's third stage relates to reentry into the home culture on furlough, retirement, or resignation.[13]

Encountering Resistance on the Field

Added to the mixture of stress-causing issues lies the largest problem of any missionary family—how to connect with a people group that is resistant, if not hostile, to the gospel. The missionaries have sacrificed to be in this strange place, only to find people who may not like them and who may actually pose a danger to them because of the Christ they proclaim.

One area of resistance may come from indigenous churches. Most local believers welcome help in reaching their communities for Christ. They generally exhibit strong, sacrificial dedication to Christ and His church. In many locations, Christians and their pastors have suffered for their faith. When missionaries enter such fields, existing church leaders may eagerly receive missionaries' assistance, but feel they have earned the right to determine what sort of ministry should take place. Often, they expect the missionary to provide a support role, especially financially, and believe the missionary should defer strategy development to established leaders.

In other places, missionaries develop strong personal relationships with local leaders. They patiently prove themselves trustworthy and earn acceptance by indigenous co-laborers. Should such a partnership not be well established, missionaries can find themselves hindered by the very people they are trying to reach.

Another source of difficulty lies in national or religious rivalries. American Christian missionaries immediately have three barriers to overcome. Their first hurdle can involve being an American in a nation that may have current or historical conflicts with the United States. Another obstacle involves serving a people group whose religious culture strongly opposes any Christian influence or expression. The third strike can involve simply being a missionary—a foreign presence whose agenda may not be appreciated by a population with a very different worldview. Each of these problems can be overcome, but at best, they produce stress with which the missionary family must cope.

The Stress of Returning Home

When missionaries return home, they experience various levels of stress. Some feel guilty for leaving people whom they love, knowing that no one may take their place. They might experience grief over the loss of relationships with believers they have led to Christ and/or nurtured. Wise missions groups provide debriefing sessions to help with the missionary family's emotional, as well as physical, return from the field.[14]

Returning missionary families may be annoyed at problems in the Western culture and church. After seeing believers sacrifice for their faith on the mission field, they can lose patience with people who take their privilege for granted.

MK teens may have special difficulties dealing with lack of acceptance when they try to reintegrate into church youth groups. One MK wrote: ". . . kids are cruel and, being an MK, you are different and get singled out. The parents want to hold you up as an example for their kids, and meanwhile the kids don't know what you're talking about."[15]

Neal Priolo chronicled the stories of several returning missionary families. The degree of difficulty on returning stateside relates to the length of time on the field, the degree of change between the field and home, the change in the missionaries themselves, the attitude of the home church, the amount of preparation before returning, and the acceptance of reentry stress.[16] Readers may be troubled by the horror stories of missionaries coming home to major physical, emotional, financial, and spiritual problems without supportive congregations and families.

Each of us should be highly motivated to take action to provide for returning missionaries and their families. They need homes, jobs, transportation, and perhaps even clothing. Most of all, they need our love, respect, and open arms.

CHAPTER SIX

Methods for Managing Stress

Spiritual Methods for Managing Stress

G od does not intend for His people to merely exist and subsist; He wants us to experience abundant life through His Son, Jesus (John 10:10). Christ alone provides what each of us needs not only to manage stress, but to be victorious over whatever robs us of the kind of life He came to give. While this book shares physical, mental, emotional, and other ways to deal with stress, without the work of Christ's Spirit, we cannot begin to enter a victorious life. Jesus should be our first, not last, resort.

Enter the Spirit-Filled Life

Hudson Taylor called it the Exchanged Life. Watchman Nee called it the Normal Christian Life. Others have called it the Abundant Life or the Deeper Life. The primary way believers successfully live victoriously over sin, stress, and other problems is by entering the Spirit-filled life. Dr. Charles Solomon's counseling approach primarily guides patients to receive Christ as Savior and surrender to His Lordship in all areas of life.[1] As Bill Bright describes it, the Spirit-filled life begins when we confess our sin and place Jesus back on the throne of our lives. Yielding to Christ, we appropriate the fullness of the Spirit.[2]

Every believer receives the Holy Spirit at conversion. Paul wrote, "But ye are not in the flesh, but in the Spirit, if so be that the Spirit of God dwell in you. Now if any man has not the Spirit of Christ, he is none of his" (Romans 8:9). God's Spirit convicts us of sin, testifies of the Savior, regenerates the believer, and immerses the child of God into Christ (John 16:8, 15:26; Titus 3:5; 1 Corinthians 12:13). God wants us to experience more than just having the Spirit within our lives; He wants us to be filled with His Spirit.

Having Christ at the center of life allows one to be filled continuously with the Spirit (Ephesians 5:18). Living within the believer, the Spirit of God produces spiritual fruit—love, joy, peace, patience, kindness, goodness, faith, gentleness, and self-control (Galatians 5:22). Stress cannot overcome someone who continually experiences the fruit of the indwelling Spirit of God.

The key to entering the Spirit-filled, Christ-controlled life is consecration, according to Hannah Whitehall Smith in her classic book *The Christian's Secret of a Happy Life*. Consecration is nothing less than abandonment to the Lord in all things.[3] Studies of many great Christians reveal how God brought them to a spiritual crisis in which they were forced to choose between continuing in the struggles of the flesh or surrendering completely to Christ. The Holy Spirit cannot fill us if we have not yielded every part of our lives to Him. Repentance of sin and receiving the Spirit's filling by faith also comprise the path to the continual filling of the Holy Spirit.

Hannah Smith calls this the "life hid with Christ in God." She adds, ". . . the Scriptures set before the believer in the Lord Jesus a life of abiding rest and of continual victory, which is far beyond the ordinary run of Christian experience. . . . We have presented to us a Savior able to save us from the power of our sins as really as He saves us from their guilt."[4]

Abide in Christ

Isolation on the mission field, spiritually as well as socially, means the missionary family must be deliberate in maintaining their walk with Christ. Constantly giving to others requires constant refueling. Missionary to China Lottie Moon literally starved herself to death by giving her food to the hungry seekers gathered around her each day. Modern missionaries can do the same spiritually if they do not diligently gain spiritual nourishment by abiding in Christ, the Vine from Whom all spiritual fruit comes.

Kane urges missionary families to feed their souls by maintaining a quiet time, reading the Bible devotionally (not merely for sermon or lesson preparation), retreating to prayer regularly, reading devotional literature, observing family devotions, taking advantage of conferences with other missionaries, and enjoying spiritual music.[5]

In addition, where possible, missionaries should be part of a local church congregation, not merely to minister but to allow the church to minister to them. Spiritual formation provides a vital role in missionaries' personal development and their ability to overcome sin and stress.

Rediscover Prayer

In His most stress-filled hour, Jesus prayed. Before His arrest and crucifixion, He prayed (Matthew 26:36–44). On the cross, He prayed (Luke 23:33–34, 46). Jesus' habit of prayer gives believers a wonderful example to follow. Jesus prayed regularly. He often resorted to a solitary place to commune with the Father. "And in the morning, rising up a great while before day, he went out, and departed into a solitary place, and there prayed" (Mark 1:35). In the Sermon on the Mount, He taught His disciples not to be worried about their daily needs, but to trust their heavenly Father and share their concerns with Him in prayer (Matthew 6:5–15, 25–34).

Unfortunately, prayer is one of the first spiritual acts to suffer when facing anxiety. Instead of going to the Father with our concerns, worries, and fears, we tend to withdraw from God as well as people. Once we determine to cast away a victim mentality and begin managing our stress, the first step is to reconnect with the Lord through prayer. If we want to trade anxiety for a peace that passes all understanding, we have only to bring every concern to God in prayer and supplication, offering thanksgiving at the same time as an act of faith that God hears and responds (Philippians 4:6–7).

The Father loves to hear His children pray through the name of His Son. "Hitherto have ye asked nothing in my name: ask, and ye shall receive, that your joy may be full" (John 16:24). When we receive Christ, we are placed in Him, and He comes to live within us through His Spirit. Praying in Jesus' name means more than adding a signature phrase to the end of our prayers. To pray in Christ's name involves reckoning our position in the Father's family through the Son and to pray as He would. The substance and the spirit of prayer cease to be our own and meld with the intercession of the Son Himself.

As we revive our communion with the Father through prayer, we can share our deepest pain, our most fearsome anxieties, and our persistent doubts. He welcomes our honesty in prayer and responds with love and healing.

Repent

Regrets for wrongdoings drag believers into a morass of heartache and stress. Instead of wallowing in condemnation, repent and confess sin to the Lord Who is ready and willing to forgive and cleanse (1 John 1:9).

David understood that failure to repent condemned him to further despair. Only when we turn from our sin and return to Christ can we find freedom through His forgiveness. "When I kept silence, my bones waxed old through my roaring all the day long. For day and night your hand was heavy upon me: my moisture is turned into the drought of summer. I acknowledged my sin unto you, and my iniquity have I not hid. I said, I will confess my transgressions unto the LORD; and you forgave the iniquity of my sin. Selah" (Psalm 32:3–5).

Friends may need to intervene and confront associates with their need for repentance and a renewed relationship with Christ. The apostle Paul took that approach with the church at Corinth. He wrote a strongly worded letter urging them to repent. They appear to have done so because his second letter refers to the results of repentance: "For though I made you sorry with a letter, I do not repent, though I did repent: for I perceive that the same epistle hath made you sorry, though it were but for a season. Now I rejoice, not that you were made sorry, but that you sorrowed to repentance: for you were made sorry after a godly manner, that you might receive damage by us in nothing. For godly sorrow works repentance to salvation not to be repented of: but the sorrow of the world works death" (2 Corinthians 7:8–10).

Forgive and Accept Forgiveness

Receiving Christ's forgiveness removes one of the strongest sources of stress—sin. Forgiving others eliminates another cause of stress—anger and bitterness. We forgive not because others deserve it, but because God, for Christ's sake, has forgiven us (Ephesians 4:32). Jude prayed that God would multiply mercy, peace, and love in their lives (Jude 1:2). Few actions

can relieve stress as experiencing and expressing mercy toward others and/
or oneself.

One international evangelist carried a long-time burden of anger
toward people who hurt him as he grew up. Harboring bitterness toward
former teachers, coaches, and even his father, hindered his effectiveness
and brought him under constant conviction. Finally, he accepted the Holy
Spirit's aid and completely surrendered his anger. One by one, he forgave
each person. Having forgiven, he also had to accept God's forgiveness. The
freedom he received afterward allowed him to experience the fullness of
the Holy Spirit's empowerment for service. God blessed his ministry as he
preached with new joy and liberty.

Observe the Sabbath

Jesus said man was not made for the Sabbath, but rather the Sabbath
was made for man. People need a rest. Just as Jesus told His followers to
"come ye apart," even so, modern disciples need to take time away from
the work. God designed human bodies, minds, and spirits to need a day a week for rest and refreshment—spiritually and physically. Neglecting this physical and spiritual principle prevents families from recovering after stressful activities and experiences.

> *"Lord, give me such a vision as will save me from mistaking a busy life for a fruitful life..."*
>
> *Eric Alexander*

Dr. Esther Schubert
referenced a prayer by Rev. Eric Alexander of Glasgow: "Lord, give me
such a vision as will save me from mistaking a busy life for a fruitful life..."[6]
Missionaries should plan some vacation annually, a Sabbath weekly, and flex
time daily. Families need quality time together for rest and recuperation.
Husbands and wives find their marriages and families strengthened as they
step away from demanding schedules and focus on each other and their
children. MKs also need time for recreation, as well as interaction with each
other and their families.

Combat Fear with Faith

Isaiah received a powerful encouragement during his ministry that has strong implications for believers today: "Fear thou not; for I am with thee: be not dismayed; for I am thy God: I will strengthen thee; yea, I will help thee; yea, I will uphold thee with the right hand of my righteousness" (Isaiah 41:10). We can overcome fear when we remember the presence of God. He does not send us to the work alone, but is always with us (Matthew 28:20). We, too, need to remember the Person Who is with us—He is our God. Think about that! The Creator of the universe is our Father and our God! We do not have a mindless, powerless idol but a living, omnipotent Lord!

Isaiah also received the promise of God's power. The Lord strengthens us for the task, empowering His children with the indwelling Holy Spirit. When our strength slacks, He comes alongside us and helps us. At the end of our abilities, He lifts us up with His right hand of righteousness.

Faith is the opposite of fear and anxiety. Experiencing stressful emotions should motivate us to reexamine and reaffirm our faith in God. If we believe that He cares for us, we should be able to cast our cares on Him, having faith that He cares for us (1 Peter 5:7).

- **Faith Expressed in Prayer.** Our first response to stressful situations should be to pray. Nothing puts us into clarifying communion with Christ as does prayer. Paul encouraged believers, "Be anxious for nothing, but in everything by prayer and supplication with thanksgiving let your requests be made known to God, and the peace that passes all understanding will guard your hearts and minds through Jesus Christ our Lord" (Philippians 4:6–7). Bringing our concerns to the Lord in prayer expresses faith that He hears us, that He cares for us, and that He is competent to deal with whatever we are facing.

- **Faith Expressed in Obedience.** Andrew Murray reminded us that "obedience is born of faith and that faith enables us to obey God."[7] Obedience aids stress management by putting us into the center of God's will. We may not feel like obeying, but we obey anyway. Obedience verifies our faith. If we believe, we will submit to God's direction, trusting that He knows and wants what is best for us. Jesus said that our obedience demonstrates love for Him (John 14:15). Love and faith go hand in hand. Both are keys to overcoming the pressures of life.

Embrace Hope

Stress can be managed more effectively if people anticipate a positive outcome. Instead of allowing troubles to discourage and stress us, we can rejoice in the midst of difficult times. Paul wrote: ". . . we glory in tribulations also: knowing that tribulation work patience; and patience, experience; and experience, hope . . ." (Romans 5:3–4).

David Livingstone, missionary to Africa, endured severe conditions, isolation, and the loss of his wife but refused to give up. He said, "Nothing earthly will make me give up my work in despair." His example of a hopeful life continues to encourage generations of missionaries following his path into the neediest areas of our world.

We have hope because on our worst day, Jesus is still Lord and our salvation is secure. We have hope because God is still sovereign and works all things for the good of those who love Him (Romans 8:28). We have hope because the Holy Spirit lives within God's children and empowers us to live abundantly. We have hope because we are more than conquerors through Him who loves us (Romans 8:37).

Experience Love

Loving God, others, and even ourselves is the ultimate method for dealing with stress. Peace and love go hand in hand. "There is no fear in love; but perfect love casts out fear: because fear has torment. He that fears is not made perfect in love." Being able to love emanates from being loved. We are able to love God "because He first loved us" (1 John 4:18–19).

God also puts other people into our lives who love us. Each member of the missionary family should share love with each other, their coworkers, and the people whom they serve. Sometimes, stressed individuals may not feel loved or loveable. Rejecting this lie of their enemy, believers should accept that God unconditionally loved us enough for His Son "to be the propitiation for our sins" (1 John 4:10). Living in His love, we can love and be loved.

Be Content with Where God Has Placed You

John Piper has noted that if you are satisfied with Jesus, you will be satisfied with the place Jesus put you.[8] Unfortunately, some ministers become displeased with their status in life and with the location of their work. They may experience disappointment with results, disharmony with people, or distress over living conditions. They may have thought they would have moved up the power ladder of their agency, only seemingly to be forgotten in some out-of-the-way field. When tempted to be displeased with God and the location He has given us, we may well remember the story of Gregory the Illuminator.

Gregory was a third-century son of a politician who became a Christian. The king, angry at Gregory and his father, put Gregory into a pitlike dungeon sunk over twenty feet into the ground, with only a small opening at the surface. Rain provided his only water. Each day an elderly woman dropped a bit of food through the opening. He lived for twelve years in his own filth. One day the king became sick. Unable to find a cure among the physicians and magicians, the king recalled the holy man in the pit. Standing again above ground, Gregory chose to forgive and pray for the king. God heard the prayer and healed the potentate. In response, the king declared Gregory's God to be the one true God and his country, Armenia, to be a Christian nation.

If we knew God would accomplish His purpose through us, might we not be more content where God places us? The apostle Paul found himself in palaces and prisons. He knew abundance and abasement. Yet, he had learned "in whatsoever state I am, therein to be content." He could not do so on his own, but he could do "all things through Christ" (Philippians 4:11–13).

Fearlessly Engage in Spiritual Warfare

Spiritual warfare accompanies every believer's experience, but missionary families are especially subject to the attack of the evil one. The devil definitely does not like what they are doing and will use any means necessary to harm them. Only by a strong walk with the Lord can believers find the spiritual power to overcome their enemy. A vital part of spiritual preparation involves teaching all members of the family how to recognize and deal with spiritual assaults.

Steven Lawson's book, *Faith Under Fire*, gives numerous ways adults can stand against the enemy.[9] One additional place parents must stand their ground is in intercessory prayer for their children and teenagers. Praying for and with them on a constant, regular basis provides a persistent appeal before the throne of heaven. It also models for the young people how they should pray for themselves and each other. Interceding for your children helps them understand just how much you love them. In addition, hearing Mom and Dad pray for them with passionate resolve and confident faith gives teens and children a sense of confidence as they deal with whatever difficulties or temptations they might experience.

Mental Methods for Managing Stress

Acknowledge Christ's Power

Many secular approaches to stress management emphasize taking control of one's situation. Self-effort and mental gymnastics constitute a useless act of psychocybernetics without the aid of the Holy Spirit. Instead of merely claiming personal power during a crisis, acknowledge Christ's power over every situation.

Affirm each passage as they testify to Christ's ability. He is an omnipotent God and has ultimate authority and power over every aspect of existence. Jesus has all power in heaven and earth. (Matthew 28:18). Everything, including those matters that threaten our lives, have been put under His feet (Ephesian 1:22; Hebrews 2:8).

Speaking helps solidify mental affirmation. Verbalize Scripture that proclaims God's superiority over whatever the problem may be. He is more than able to handle every challenge confronting us. He is able to save those who are tempted (Hebrews 2:18). He is able to keep us from falling (Jude 1:24). He is able to keep what we have committed to Him (2 Timothy 1:12). He is able to do exceedingly abundantly above all we could ask or think (Ephesians 3:20).

Reeducate Yourself to Think Biblically

How one thinks as well as what one thinks is vital to mental health and maintaining a positive spiritual attitude. We are called to be transformed by the renewing of our minds. One of the best ways to experience a transformed mind is to think about good and godly matters. Paul wrote: "Finally, brethren, whatsoever things are true, whatsoever things are honest, whatsoever things are just, whatsoever things are pure, whatsoever things are lovely, whatsoever things are of good report; if there be any virtue, and if there be any praise, think on these things" (Philippians 4:8).

Eliminate sources of temptation, whether television, movies, music, books, or Internet content that is ungodly. Place a filter on the computer's Internet programs to help family members avoid harmful websites. Develop mutual accountability both within the family and between family members and peers on the mission field.

Learn to think biblically. Larry Crabb teaches that stressed emotions proceed from sinful behavior, which in turn comes from unbiblical beliefs (thinking). After discovering the source of incorrect patterns of thinking, he reeducates patients by teaching them biblical truth. When our beliefs and ways of approaching issues are based on Scripture, we behave differently—following biblical patterns of life, which produce positive emotions.[10]

Quietly Meditate on God's Word

Secular stress therapy emphasizes the value of meditation but lacks a spiritual basis. It usually defaults to Eastern mysticism and yoga. Christians should not reject the notion of using meditation but should meditate in a biblical way—focusing on God and His Word. While Eastern meditation tells practitioners to empty their minds, Christian meditation instructs us to fill our minds with the Word of God. The psalmist wrote: "But his delight is in the law of the LORD; and in his law doth he meditate day and night. And he shall be like a tree planted by the rivers of water, that brings forth his fruit in his season; his leaf also shall not wither; and whatsoever he doeth shall prosper" (Psalm 1:2–3). By memorizing Scripture and focusing our thoughts on God's Word, we internalize the very thoughts of Christ.

Effective contemplation requires a degree of silence and solitude, both rare commodities in the missionary context. Jesus often left the disciples and went into an isolated place to pray (Luke 6:12). Spending all night in prayer with His Father was not unusual for Christ. When ministry demands became so constant that He and the disciples did not have enough time for a meal, Jesus called them to "come apart and rest for a while" (Mark 6:31).

In a home with children, quiet times require discipline and creativity. Escaping the stressful distraction of noise may mean rising somewhat earlier than the rest of the family or staying up after others have gone to bed.

Focus Your Mind on the Lord

Whatever is the object of constant attention impacts our minds, dragging us toward that focus like a magnet. If we constantly think about money, or the lack of it, we become materialistic. If we obsess over our physical well-being, we can become hypochondriacs. Paul urged believers: "Set your affection on things above, not on things on the earth" (Colossians 3:2). The Greek word translated as *affection* literally means "to exercise the mind." The apostle knew the benefit of focusing his mind on eternal matters rather than the temporal issues of this world.

When our hearts and minds center on Christ, other issues slide down the ladder of importance. Instead of being captive to changing circumstances, our spiritual center frees us to think more clearly and biblically. We are able to approach problems with Spirit-directed rationality. Holding the things of this earth very loosely, we are liberated to follow Christ's leadership without the anchors of life dragging us down.

Tim and his family left the comforts of home in the American South to live in a country that was hostile to Christians. After several years, they were able to reach a number of seekers with the Good News of Christ. Settling into a new culture, they adopted this people group as their own. Unexpectedly, a major political and religious shift created a dangerous environment for Christians, especially American expatriates. Tim and his family had to leave the region quickly, leaving nearly all of their belongings behind.

Tim's family was more deeply affected by having to leave their friends and the new believers they had led to Christ than they were at losing their earthly possessions. Sure, it was hard. Nearly a lifetime of photos, personal items, and memories were gone. Yet, because they had committed themselves to Christ and focused their affections and minds on Him, they were able to endure the stress and sorrow of the moment. They knew greater matters were at hand and gave themselves patiently to see where God would take them next.

Embrace Contentment

Stress often arises when we lack contentment. We covet something we do not have. We want to be somewhere besides the place where we are. We desire a position beyond our reach, power beyond our abilities, or prestige beyond our talents. Instead of being grateful for God's wisdom in placing us where we are and giving us what we have, we become resentful that others have what we do not.

Paul learned to be content in whatever state he found himself (Philippians 4:13). Contentment does not mean to be satisfied with the status quo and not desire something better—for ourselves, our families, or our ministries. Contentment involves being at rest mentally, emotionally, and spiritually. Instead of experiencing angst or anger over circumstances beyond our control, we are able to receive whatever God places into our lives with grace and acceptance.

> *Contentment involves being at rest mentally, emotionally, and spiritually. Instead of experiencing angst or anger over circumstances beyond our control, we are able to receive whatever God places into our lives with grace and acceptance.*

Paul passed his secret of contentment on to his protégé Timothy, advising him that "godliness with contentment is great gain. For we brought nothing into this world, and it is certain we can carry nothing out. And having food and raiment let us be therewith content" (1 Timothy 6:6–8). Timothy learned he could consider godliness and contentment a worthy objective in life.

Finally, Paul reminds us that we cannot accomplish this state of contentment through our own abilities. Our fleshly nature resists it. The forces of a worldly system conspire against it. Still, we can do this and all things through Christ Who strengthens us (Philippians 4:13).

Accentuate the Positive

Insomnia and worry are twin enemies. Generally, both result from focusing on problems—past, present, or future. Having a mindset that gravitates toward the negative makes matters worse. Pessimists usually anticipate events turning out poorly, people behaving badly toward them, and life in general ending disappointingly. Negativity breeds stress. Pessimists not only suffer from bad things that happen to them, but they also suffer from bad things that *might* happen.

Instead of dwelling on the negative, accentuate the positive. When confronting a problem, begin with the realization that your Father is Lord of all, including this problem. Believing the Lord is quite capable of dealing with whatever comes your way, you can trust Him and start anticipating a good outcome. Even if matters do not turn out as you wish, you will deal with the results with the strength and support of God.

Christians should follow the advice of that familiar hymn by Johnson Oatman:

"When upon life's billows you are tempest-tossed,
When you are discouraged, thinking all is lost,
Count your many blessings, name them one by one,
And it will surprise you what the Lord hath done." [11]

Developing a positive attitude does not mean adopting an idealistic, fantasy approach to genuinely difficult problems. It does not mean putting on rose-colored glasses to filter out very ugly, painful realities. Instead, a positive mindset involves choosing to trust God regardless of what may come. This way of thinking sees God has worked in our lives and believes He can do it again. With His strength, we can tune our minds toward faith instead of doubt, courage instead of fear, and anticipation instead of regret.

Have Faith in God

Many people struggling with stress try to resolve difficulties in their own power. They rely on mental acuity, financial accumulations, human networks, or personal abilities to determine how they should live. While nothing is wrong with employing every available resource, our trust cannot reside in ourselves, but in the Lord.

Human understanding is limited by its very nature. We do not know what lies ahead. At best, we can rationalize, strategize, systematize, and organize. Yet, our stress levels remain constant because we cannot control the future.

Proverbs advises us to "Trust in the LORD with all your heart; and lean not unto your own understanding. In all your ways acknowledge him, and he shall direct thy paths" (Proverbs 3:5–6). Instead of relying on human understanding, we place our trust in the Lord totally. The phrase "with all your heart" means completely, absolutely. This proverb promises that when we place our lives in God's hands, acknowledging Him in every aspect of life, then He will direct our paths.

Psalm 23 has a wonderfully comforting phrase: "He leads me in the paths of righteousness for His name's sake." When we totally trust Him and commit ourselves to unreserved obedience, God's name goes on the line. His reputation is at stake. So, we do not need to worry about whether or whither He leads. He will lead. He will lead in the right ways. His name guarantees it.

Cultivating faith in God not only affects our minds and emotions, it even has benefits for our physical well-being. The rest of the passage in Proverbs 3 talks about trusting God and refusing evil: "It shall be health to thy navel, and marrow to thy bones" (Proverbs 3:8).

Emotional Methods for Managing Stress

People who can develop habits of expressing positive emotions during stressful times tend to be more stress resistant and healthy. Obviously, people do better whenever they can employ humor, rest, or even recreation to divert negative reactions and seize positive directions.

Focus Your Heart on God

Where is your heart? Not your blood pumper. Where is the seat of your affections? What really matters to you? How have you established your personal value system? When our hearts focus on things of this world, we set ourselves up for stress. We spend our time and attention on matters over which we have limited control. At any point, whatever we love in this world can be taken away from us. Consequently, worry, fear, and other negative emotions run rampant through our hearts.

When our affections are focused on the things of God, we count material possessions only to be of such value as they can be used in His service. David greatly desired to build a house (temple) for the Lord. God refused David's plan, but allowed Solomon to build the first temple. David told his son that because he had set his affection on the house of the Lord, he had set aside large amounts of gold, silver, and other precious materials for the house of God (1 Chronicles 29:3).

Having our treasure in heaven, we do not cling to the things of earth and are less stressed by their loss (Matthew 6:19–21). As Paul said, "They that are Christ's have crucified the flesh with the affections and lusts" (Galatians 5:24). Our emotions are liberated because they are pining for heaven, not pinned to the earth.

If we focus our hearts on God, emotions stabilize because they have a firm foundation. Paul prayed for the Thessalonians: "And the Lord direct your hearts into the love of God, and into the patient waiting for Christ" (2 Thessalonians 3:5). Love for God goes hand in hand with the steadfastness of Christ.

Cultivate Tranquility

Proverbs teaches us "A sound heart is the life of the flesh: but envy the rottenness of the bones" (Proverbs 14:30). The Hebrew word translated *sound* refers not to physical health (although a physically healthy heart is a very good thing!); instead, it carries the connotation of tranquility. How do we cultivate tranquility? By trusting Christ.

Personal peace comes ultimately from Jesus. He gives His followers a peace that is different from what can be found from worldly sources: "Peace I leave with you, my peace I give unto you: not as the world gives, give I unto you. Let not your heart be troubled, neither let it be afraid" (John 14:27). Temporary relief may be found from meditation or medication, but permanent peace proceeds only from the Prince of Peace.

Focus on Jesus and bring all your cares to the Lord. A tranquil mind and heart emerge from consistent communion with Christ. When stressful burdens seem ready to break through and destroy your peace, bring your care to Jesus, casting all your care on Him, knowing He cares for you (1 Peter 5:7).

Persistent prayer helps us keep our relationship with Jesus fresh and vital. Talk with Him about what is going on in your life as you would your best friend. Paul urged, "Be careful (anxious) for nothing; but in everything by prayer and supplication with thanksgiving let your requests be made known unto God. And the peace of God, which passes all understanding, shall keep your hearts and minds through Christ Jesus" (Philippians 4:6–7). Prayer is not merely a pipeline for divine blessings; it allows God's children to crawl up on His lap and cry "Abba, Father," with all the trust and love such an act entails.

Interject Fun into Your Family's Schedule

"All work and no play makes Jack a dull boy," according to the old proverb. Scripture reminds us that "a merry heart does good like medicine . . ." (Proverbs 17:22). Whether engaging in a hobby, playing with the family, or simply appreciating the quiet company of good friends over a meal, finding godly ways to enjoy life is not sinful; it is necessary.

Children are not the only members of the missionary family who need to have fun. The entire family needs personal and interactive opportunities for enjoyable interaction. We're familiar with the truth "The family that prays together stays together." They also need to play together. Activities do not have to be extravagant or expensive. Simple table games, hikes, picnics outdoors, or even an occasional game of chase around the house can bring smiles to faces and ease stress from hearts.

One missionary wrote, "Being a missionary is a serious call, but it doesn't mean you can't have fun. One of my goals is to play golf or watch a movie once per month just because it helps me to relax a little more. My wife and I go on a date at least once every two weeks and that also helps a great deal in relating well to each other. I think for the kids, especially, it is vital for them to see their parents enjoying life and be thankful regardless of where they are living."

Missionary work is serious, but the missionary life should not be a constant burden. When unbelievers observe Christians, they should see a vital, healthy lifestyle. Enjoying life does not mean one degenerates into frivolity, but neither does spirituality mean one goes around with a sad and serious countenance all the time. Finding ways simply to enjoy the life Christ has given us can help relieve tension and lift the spirits.

Learn to Laugh

"All the days of the afflicted are evil: but he that is of a merry heart hath a continual feast" (Proverbs 15:15). Approaching life with a good sense of humor helps ease tension and put matters into perspective. Spirituality does not require a somber countenance. To the contrary, the fruit of the Spirit includes joy! One does not have to become a stand-up comedian to combat stressful situations, but seeing the humorous side of matters may provide the emotional relief to handle arduous challenges.

> *Spirituality does not require a somber countenance. To the contrary, the fruit of the Spirit includes joy!*

What others see in our faces generates from our hearts. Proverbs teaches, "A merry heart makes a cheerful countenance: but by sorrow of the heart the spirit is broken" (Proverbs 15:13). When children see parents' worried expressions, they worry as well. Conversely, when Mom and Dad habitually smile and laugh, the kids generally feel happy and secure. One does not have to hide genuine concern behind fake grins. Children, and especially teens, can spot a phony from a mile away. However, the normal tone of life in missionary homes ought to include plenty of joy, gladness, and merrymaking.

Accept Your Acceptance

Many people feel rejected. I've interviewed many ministers who had lifelong problems because a father or mother only offered conditional acceptance—giving approval solely when the child performed well. One young preacher wept as he recalled growing up never feeling that he met his father's expectations. If he made an A on a test, his father questioned why he did not make an A+. If he won the silver medal at the school track meet, the look on Dad's face made it clear he should have won gold. As a result, he never felt accepted except when he excelled in everything he did. Unconditional love and acceptance does not mean avoiding any hint of encouragement to excellence. Rather, it involves loving someone just as they are, regardless of achievement.

Dr. Charles Solomon calls this the rejection syndrome. Solomon encourages believers to die to self and accept their position in Christ. Accept the fact that we are "accepted in the Beloved" (Ephesians 1:6). Being "in Christ" we do not have to worry about seeking approval from others because our Father gives us His unconditional love through His Son.[12]

When asked what was impacting his life in his later years, Dr. Dallas Demmit said he was "learning to live loved." Some people find it hard to accept love. Missionaries are quick to give love but sometimes feel unworthy of receiving it. Living in the love of God and fellow believers is critical to a healthy approach to the Christian life.

Every member of the missionary family needs expressions of acceptance for one another. Parents must not assume their children know they love them. MKs need to be told "I love you," just like any other child or teenager. (By the way—Kids, your parents need to hear those precious three words from you too.) Missionary wives need to hear sweet words of affirmation from their husbands and vice versa.

Sometimes, family members do their best to demonstrate their love and acceptance, but some people have difficulty accepting their acceptance. Often, guilt for some past deed may prevent acceptance of love or even of forgiveness. Emotional self-flagellation may be a poor attempt at making up for hidden sins. Shame strongly deters a sense of approval, leaving victims feeling unworthy of others' love.

We need to realize we are not accepted because we have nothing in our past worthy of guilt or shame. Our acceptance is not conditioned on our actions at all. We are accepted "in the Beloved." When we trust Christ, repenting of sin and receiving Him as Savior, we are placed "in Christ" (Galatians 3:27). Our past slate is wiped clean, and we are remade as new creations in Christ (2 Corinthians 5:17). Our acceptance does not depend on us but on Christ. If the Father accepts us on the merits of His Son, we should not insult Him by refusing to accept our acceptance.

Listen to Good Music

David's harp and hymns soothed Saul's troubled heart (1 Samuel 6:14–23). Even so, soothing and inspirational music can ease stressed emotions. Lyrics from good Christian songs encourage faith and hope. Worship-oriented music elevates the spirit, inviting listeners to focus on the Lord instead of troubles. Instrumental recordings can provide relaxing backgrounds, calming the emotions.

On many mission fields, Internet accessibility allows families to enjoy online music or radio programs. They can purchase songs to be played on mp3 players as they travel. Where such convenience is not available, stateside families and friends might supply missionaries with good CDs or other sources of music. Christians in many countries have developed deeply moving Christian music in their languages, reflecting the style and mood of the national culture.

At the same time, music or any other emotional ointment does not heal the source of the stress. Dr. Jay Adams points out that Saul's relief was only temporary: "Saul's own attitudes and actions kept making his condition worse, as day by day he brooded with jealousy and resentment." Adams notes that Saul's problem was sin.[13] When sin is the root of stress, only repentance and forgiveness can provide long-term relief.

Sing

God inhabits the praise of His people (Psalm 22:3). We experience God's presence when our songs transform mournful expressions of grief over into praise of the Most High God, our Deliverer. Joy comes in realizing His love, mercy, and grace. Stress melts away under the glow of praise sung to our Savior.

David, the "sweet singer of Israel," not only wrote scores of songs (known as the Psalms), he obviously sang them. Many psalms must have been soulful ballads, written when David was hiding from his enemies. You can hear the pathos in his words as he offers his prayers to the Lord. Imagine David hiding in the cliff caves of eastern Israel, worried about his kingdom and angry over unjust attacks. His men likely listened in the night as he sang those prayers of faith.

Missionaries can enhance family worship by singing praise to the Lord. Since each generation loves to sing songs of their youth, a variety of songs can be experienced. Children and teenagers like music familiar to their age groups. Older people may not know the newer songs, but each generation can join the other in praise through music.

As several families joined together at a house in central Asia, worship began with a young adult leading the children in songs appropriate to their age. The leader then transitioned to music more familiar to the teens present. The final group of songs included a blend of standard hymns and contemporary praise choruses. Each person's eyes lit up as they sang, experiencing personal worship to the Lord.

Singing can often be best when one is alone. You do not have to have an audience or others singing along with you. Whether driving from place to place, walking along the way, or simply sitting at home, singing can change one's mood from sadness to gladness. As the Holy Spirit begins to fill one's heart, the natural expression involves "Speaking to yourselves in psalms and hymns and spiritual songs, singing and making melody in your heart to the Lord" (Ephesians 5:19).

Develop Stress-Resistant Attitudes

Some people seem to be more stress resistant than others. They have just as many stress-causing incidents in their lives as others do, but they display remarkable resilience. Part of the reason lies in their ability to use good attitudes to shape their emotions, rather than allowing their emotions to rule their lives.

Miranda Ferrara observed several common factors for stress-resistant personalities:

1. They view change as a challenging and normal part of life, rather than as a threat.
2. They have a sense of control over their lives, believe that setbacks are temporary, and believe they will succeed if they work toward their goals.
3. They have commitments to work, family, friends, and have support systems.
4. They engage in regular activities that promote relaxation [14]

In addition to these qualities, people wanting to increase their ability to overcome stress should intentionally groom their attitudes according to scriptural principles. For example, the apostle Paul saw God's hand behind everything that entered his life. Therefore, although he had been beaten and thrown into a dungeon, he and his coworker, Silas, were able to pray and sing praise to the Lord in the middle of the night (Acts 16:25). They may have been prisoners, but their hearts were not captive to their circumstances because their attitudes had been shaped by Christ.

Behavioral Methods for Managing Stress

Live with Integrity

When threatened on every side, King David relied on the mercy of God and pled that he had maintained his integrity even in spite of wicked attacks (Psalm 26). Sometimes, people under stress are tempted to take shortcuts morally or ethically. In their weariness, they are susceptible to the lure of whatever makes them feel better. Maintaining integrity enables believers to receive God's healing. "Be not wise in thine own eyes: fear the LORD, and depart from evil. It shall be health to thy navel, and marrow to thy bones" (Proverbs 3:7–8).

Since sin and duplicity lead directly to a stress-filled life, the best path toward peace follows the straight path of integrity. When you speak honestly and lovingly, you need not worry about what you said to whom. When you act properly and with good intention, you need not fear what someone might think. When you exercise integrity in each area of life, you can experience the tranquility of the upright in heart (Psalm. 10:7).

Depend on God and Wait Patiently on Him

Sometimes the best thing to do is—nothing. Yet, nothing is not always nothing. Waiting on God involves actively trusting Him to work in your life in His way and time. Instead of trying to take control of a stressful situation that appears beyond you, turn the circumstance over to the Lord. "He gives power to the faint; and to them that have no might he increases strength. Even the youths shall faint and be weary, and the young men shall utterly fall: But they that wait upon the LORD shall renew their strength; they shall mount up with wings as eagles; they shall run, and not be weary; and they shall walk, and not faint" (Isaiah 40:29–31).

Act, Take Proactive Steps

Stress tends to paralyze its victims. People experiencing prolonged stress may feel helpless to deal with their problems. Taking proactive steps toward ameliorating the situation produces positive emotions and hope. Jay Adams argues that behaving in a biblical manner affects our emotions in a positive way.[15] He refers to God's encounter with Cain who was depressed

117

over the rejection of his offering. God responded, "If you do well, shall you not be accepted?" (Genesis 4:7).

Build Positive Relationships

Positive relationships not only help us manage stress, but when we apply love in all interactions, we reduce the sources of stress. Certainly, we need to enjoy and strengthen friendships with people who care for us. However, Jesus taught: "Love your enemies, bless them that curse you, do good to them that hate you, and pray for them which despitefully use you, and persecute you; That ye may be the children of your Father which is in heaven: . . ." (Matthew 5:44–45) When we serve others, we may be surprised that our enemies become our friends!

Scripture constantly admonishes believers to interact with one another in positive ways. This list is not exhaustive, but imagine how healthier and happier your life would be if you acted accordingly with your spouse, your children, your parents, or other people:

- "Be kindly affectioned one to another with brotherly love; in honor preferring one another" (Romans 12: 10).
- "Be of the same mind one toward another . . ." (Romans 12:16).
- "Let us therefore follow after the things which make for peace, and things wherewith one may edify another" (Romans 14:19).
- "Wherefore receive one another, as Christ also received us to the glory of God" (Romans 15:7).
- "For, brethren, you have been called unto liberty; only use not liberty for an occasion to the flesh, but by love serve one another" (Galatians 5:13).
- "And be kind one to another, tenderhearted, forgiving one another, even as God for Christ's sake has forgiven you" (Ephesians 4:32).
- "Submitting yourselves one to another in the fear of God" (Ephesians 5:21).
- "Forbearing one another, and forgiving one another, if any man have a quarrel against any: even as Christ forgave you, so also do you" (Colossians 3:13).
- "Wherefore comfort yourselves together, and edify one another, even as also you do" (1 Thessalonians 5:11).

These admonitions and others can be summed up in Jesus' command to His disciples, and through them to us: "A new commandment I give unto you, that you love one another; as I have loved you, that you also love one another. By this shall all men know that you are my disciples, if you have love one to another" (John 13:34–35).

Manage Your Time

Master a two-letter word: NO. Missionaries unnecessarily feel guilty if they do not accept every invitation, follow each opportunity, and fill their days with activity. In his book, *Margin*, Richard Swenson urges readers to build white space (uncommitted time) around their schedules.[16] Inevitably, crises emerge and without some margin of time, people quickly become overcommitted. Someone observed that Paul said, "This one thing I do," not "These forty things I dabble in." Scripture reminds us that our days are few and precious, so we should use them wisely. "So teach us to number our days, that we may apply our hearts unto wisdom" (Psalm 90:12).

Work for Jesus

Interestingly, work can be an effective behavioral approach to managing stress. Certainly, many people experience stress due to employment situations and their reactions to it. However, work itself is part of life. Work can be a blessing or a bane depending on one's attitude. Work involves more than mere employment. We work at home; we work at hobbies; we work at raising children. In every aspect of life, we work. The key is not working for ourselves, or even just for the employer, but for the Lord (Colossians 3:23).

Work was not part of the Curse related to the Fall in the Garden of Eden. Prior to Adam and Eve's sin, God said unto them, "Be fruitful, and multiply, and replenish the earth, and subdue it: and have dominion over the fish of the sea, and over the fowl of the air, and over every living thing that moves upon the earth" (Genesis 1:27–28). Humankind was intended to be good stewards of God's creation. In fact, in creating, God worked: "And on the seventh day God ended his work which he had made; and he rested on the seventh day from all his work which he had made" (Genesis 2:2).

Sin's judgment caused toil to become difficult: ". . . cursed is the ground for your sake; in sorrow shall you eat of it all the days of your life; Thorns also and thistles shall it bring forth to you; and you shalt eat the herb of the field; In the sweat of your face shall you eat bread, till you return unto the ground . . ." (Genesis 3:17–19).

Scripture admonishes believers to be diligent in work. Using an agricultural example, Proverbs encourages us to be diligent in our work: "Be thou diligent to know the state of thy flocks, and look well to thy herds" (Proverbs 27:23). Illustrating from nature, Scripture goes on to urge responsible work while warning against the results of laziness: "Go to the ant, you sluggard; consider her ways, and be wise: Which having no guide, overseer, or ruler, provides her meat in the summer, and gathers her food in the harvest. How long will you sleep, O sluggard? When will you arise out of your sleep? Yet a little sleep, a little slumber, a little folding of the hands to sleep: So shall your poverty come as one that travails, and your want as an armed man" (Proverbs 6:6–11).

God's Word offers many principles and promises related to work. Joyfully engaging in productive work provides a positive approach to handling stress. When we do well in our work, our emotions rise, our finances generally improve, and we gain in self-respect. On the other hand, if we are lazy, instead of relieving stress, we add to it. "He also that is slothful in his work is brother to him that is a great waster" (Proverbs 18:9).

Invest in Others

Stress often results as we focus on ourselves. Conversely, we reduce stress by committing our attention to helping others, being friends, meeting needs, or other activities that benefit someone other than ourselves. Seeing God bless another person through your ministry produces powerful feelings of satisfaction. While being careful not to claim God's glory as He touches others, we can experience inner joy as we watch their response to His grace.

Everyone in the missionary family can find ways to help other people. Wives can encourage other women, offering words and works of encouragement. A fellow worker may need a listening ear. A neighbor could be stressed out with sick children. An elderly church member might be struggling with physical limitations. Every day presents some opportunity for women on mission to serve someone else.

Children and teens can also become involved in serving others. What greater way to nourish their appreciation for their family's role in ministry than to participate personally in helping someone else? Sometimes MKs are very aware of their privileged position among other young people whose family may not be able to provide for them physically, financially, or spiritually.

Find a Hobby/Avocation/Recreation

While relaxation for some people involves lying in a hammock or sitting back in the easy chair for a couple of hours, stress also can be lowered by engaging in enjoyable activities such as a hobby, avocation, or other forms of recreation. Families need recreational activities to simply enjoy one another and strengthen relationships. Stress evaporates as the family enjoys playing games around the dinner table, going on a weekend trip together, watching a sports event, or sharing a mutually interesting hobby.

Be Faithful

Stress tempts sufferers to slack in their responsibilities. Physical and emotional weariness often become reasonable excuses for not making a meeting, engaging a lost neighbor in witness, helping someone in need, or following through with an assignment. Myriads of opportunities may be lost as stressed workers step back from the work. Ironically, instead of feeling less stressed, people who succumb to this temptation often feel worse. They have merely added a sense of guilt and failure to their already heavy load.

Be faithful to whatever task is at hand, even if you do not feel like doing so. Faithfulness produces a sense of satisfaction that often supersedes stress.

Be faithful to whatever task is at hand, even if you do not feel like doing so. Faithfulness produces a sense of satisfaction that often supersedes stress. Moses' leadership of a reluctant and rebellious people through desert wanderings caused him much grief, but he remained faithful. Doing what is right when things about you are going wrong produces a "Well done" from the Lord (Numbers 12:7).

Watch Your Mouth!

As you grew up, your mother may have warned you to "Watch your mouth." How we speak and how people speak to us affect our mental and emotional health. Words can even impact our physical well-being. "Pleasant

121

words are as a honeycomb, sweet to the soul, and health to the bones" (Proverbs 16:24). We cannot control others' words or actions, but we can choose to speak kindly and graciously, maintaining personal tranquility. Old and New Testament Scriptures advise us to choose words carefully.

What we say can hurt or help others as well as ourselves. Gentle words can turn aside harsh wrath (Proverbs 15:1). Good words cheer the heart (Proverbs 12:25). Pure words are pleasant (Proverbs 15:26). Well-timed words produce joy (Proverbs 15:23). "A word fitly spoken is like apples of gold in pictures of silver" (Proverbs 25:11).

Physical Methods for Managing Stress

Relax

Taking it easy is not sinful! Jesus told His disciples, "Come ye yourselves apart into a desert place, and rest a while: for there were many coming and going, and they had no leisure so much as to eat" (Mark 6:31). Having time to relax is important. Note the importance of having some leisure time and time to eat.

However, this point is more physical in nature. Stress management experts observe that just as stress causes muscle tension, deep muscle relaxation can reduce tension and, with it, control reactions to stress.[17] Sit or lie down and close your eyes. While maintaining controlled breathing, focus on each major muscle group at a time, willing each muscle to relax. Completing the easing of the entire body, one remains in a relaxed state for a period of time, continuing to breathe fully. A few minutes of deliberate physical and mental relaxation can ease both body and mind.

Exercise

Physical activity is not only healthy, but appropriate exercise releases endorphins, which elevate positive feelings. Thirty minutes of walking or other aerobic exercise three or four times a week aids physical, mental, and emotional well-being. Scripture says that bodily exercise profits a little. In his encouragement for people to focus on godliness, Paul at least acknowledged that exercise does offer positive results (1 Timothy 4:8).

Families can find ways to engage in physical activity together. Some locations are safe for hiking or walking. Both offer healthy benefits and opportunities to explore the community. Children enjoy skipping ropes, an exercise that boxers also find beneficial. Teens may prefer more challenging sports such as football or soccer. Badminton, volleyball, basketball, or other games also provide stress-relieving workouts.

Maintain Good Nutrition

Healthy living, not merely under stress, begins with solid nutrition that provides the body the vitamins, minerals, protein, carbohydrates, and good fats it needs. People experiencing stress must be careful to plan, properly prepare, and enjoy healthy foods. Since cooking often destroys important nutrients, fruits and vegetables are best when consumed raw and natural. In addition, eating in a relaxed, unhurried environment helps reduce stress and digest food.[18]

Because missionaries may not have access to healthy foods regularly, they should supplement their family's diets with multivitamins, especially Vitamin C, which aids the immune system. Note that while Christians are not bound by the dietary laws of the Old Testament, biblical guidelines for eating properly do benefit good health.

Mission-Specific Methods for Stress Management

Prepare Properly for the Missions Experience

Mission personnel who work through agencies generally receive orientation prior to leaving for the field. Training and preparation may last a few days or several weeks. Proper education regarding local culture as well as mission strategy helps mission families know in advance what to expect when they reach their assignment. Peer counseling equips missionaries with the experiences of those who have gone before them, enabling them to handle stressful circumstances more effectively.

Missionaries without solid preparation often succumb to cross-cultural crises or remain on the field, but with reduced effectiveness and ongoing loads of stress. One case study involved a layman, his wife, and teenage son who had participated in a short-term mission experience. They came away convinced God was calling them to return to that third-world country as missionaries. Selling all their possessions, they moved to their new home. However, when the wife went to the market, she was stunned at the sight of raw meat hanging in the open air, often with flies circling. Vegetables and rice was heaped on mats on the side of the road with a patina of dust from passing cars, ox carts, and bicycles. To their credit, they stayed on the field through their year-long assignment, embracing their new culture (and its food!)

Renew Your Call

Ministry is one job in which you will be absolutely miserable if you do not have the call of God. THE CALL will keep you where God wants you when nothing else will. You will want to quit, but you won't because of THE CALL. You will wonder why you didn't go to work at the factory, get that medical degree, or learn more about insurance sales. Your wife may wonder why she didn't marry Bill, or Bob, or Tom. Your children may ask why Daddy has to be away so many nights taking care of other family's problems. You may scream into the night air, "Why!" But you won't quit because of THE CALL.

One missionary and his family had spent nearly twenty years on the field. Within a short span of three years, the missionary's wife died suddenly, and all three children returned to the States to attend college. The missionary had aging parents back home. At the same time, the government of the host nation implemented harassing and very difficult visa requirements. The death of a spouse, an empty nest, and a sense of responsibility for one's parents might be enough stress to cause the missionary to call it a day and return to his own country. However, this man had a deep sense of call to his place and the people he served. He had often fasted and prayed for them. However strong the pressure, internally and externally, he was able to remain on the mission field, not stoically enduring the pain of his situation, but embracing a renewed call. This reenergized sense of purpose gave him the spiritual, mental, and emotional power to sublimate stress into new motivation for his ministry.

Find Satisfaction in Christ

Satisfaction for ministry should come not in the place of ministry, but in the person of ministry—Christ. The stress and sin of dissatisfaction can trap workers who encounter persistent resistance and few results. Particularly at midlife, some workers begin to evaluate their careers and wonder whether the outcomes have been worth the sacrifice. If they feel trapped in unsatisfying situations, they may begin to resent the very people they came to serve.

One key to overcoming the snare of discontent is to find fulfillment not in where you are or what you are doing, but in the One you serve. John Piper has said that God is most glorified when we find our satisfaction in Him. The apostle Paul testified to his personal struggle with contentment and offered the singular path to serenity: "Not that I speak in respect of want: for I have learned, in whatsoever state I am, therewith to be content. I know both how to be abased, and I know how to abound: everywhere and in all things I am instructed both to be full and to be hungry, both to abound and to suffer need. I can do all things through Christ which strengthens me" (Philippians 4:11–13).

Maintain a Strong Support System

Support systems of friends and colleagues on the field are vital to maintaining health and overcoming stress. Often, simply having someone to listen helps unload the stress and solve problems. A strong support system also involves family members, friends, and home church members. Missionaries need their prayers and encouragement. Occasional phone calls give the opportunity to talk about everyday issues and maintain relationships. (Calls today are very affordable with Skype, Magic Jack or other voice over Internet protocols, or discount phone cards). In addition, international post allows parcels of supplies, gifts, and treats to reach the missionary families for holidays, birthdays, or just to provide a bit of hometown joy.

Grandparents can provide special support for children in missionary families. These missionary kids miss the normal relationships other children have with grandparents. MK teacher, Tress Miles, reminds grandparents to give their grandchildren (and their children)

> *Grandparents can provide special support for children in missionary families. Give your children a goodbye blessing and then stay in touch.*
>
> *Tress Miles*

a goodbye blessing before they leave for the field. She encourages them to stay in touch by sending self-recorded stories, cards, birthday gifts, and other encouragements. If feasible, visiting the missionary family on the field especially aids these vital relationships and relieves the stress of living so far away from family.[19]

At the same time, friends and family should not expect the same level of contact as before. One missionary wife reported that one form of stress is trying to maintain relationships back home while nurturing relationships on the field. She wrote, "I have expectations of friends and get disappointed if I feel like I'm doing most of the initiating or feel forgotten. It's hard to juggle phone calls with the time change, I can feel torn between relationships in both places and worry that friendships will drift apart and I won't have many relationships when I go back."

Agencies also may provide on-the-field pastoral care and counseling. One agency employs fifty trained caregivers, positioned strategically around the world. These counselors include persons with pastoral care or clinical counseling credentialing, as well as practical mission experience. These caregivers regularly contact personnel in their areas. They also respond to calls for counseling and provide follow up and debriefing. Issues range from anger to depression to burnout to marriage problems to MK issues.[20]

If outside counseling becomes necessary, some agencies provide for stateside treatment at agency expense and with salary ongoing. Some missionaries take leaves of absence without pay in order to complete responsibilities and then return to the field with their agency.

Another denomination has started a new missionary care ministry. Its Missionary Care Team will be "very proactive in working with missionaries specifically relating to personal problems, one of those being stress-related issues." The National Missions Director reports: "Our goal is to have regular . . . contact with missionaries while they are on deputation, getting to the field, while on the field and during reentry, either furlough or permanent stay. Our focus will be on groups such as first-term missionaries, retiring missionaries, missionary kids, single missionaries, missionaries in specific regions, etc. We will provide counseling and or materials for grieving missionaries because of the loss of loved ones. In May of this year, we will sponsor a boot camp for our missionary team. . . . We have medical and psychological personnel to evaluate and diagnose treatment that has already been a tremendous blessing for the past few years."[21]

Build Networks

Missionaries understand the necessity of building relationships with nationals even before moving to the mission field. Certainly, most missionary families value strong friendships with other mission workers. Relating to someone of one's own language and cultural background offers the comfort of the familiar. Mutual encouragement comes through shared worship, joint prayer, and even simple events featuring meals like Mom used to make. However, many missionaries miss a blessing when they see interaction with nationals solely within the context of the mission purpose. Building networks with nationals, as well as with other missionary families, can offer support that integrates personal and professional relationships into a more normal and effective pattern.

Manage Conflict Effectively

One of the most stressful events in life is interpersonal conflict. Missionaries are not exempt from experiencing difficulties with other people. Not only do they encounter conflict in situations common to the human experience (marital or parenting conflicts, arguments with neighbors, disagreements in business dealings, etc.), they have unique circumstances that exacerbate conflict. Some workers have conflict with other missionaries over funding, methodologies, jealousies regarding support or housing, etc.

Indigenous leaders may have unrealistic expectations, perhaps thinking the American missionaries should provide more money for the nationals' personal or ministry needs. Others have racial, theological, or other bases for conflict.

Legal problems can occur when governments change residency requirements or corrupt officials demand bribes. Time and space does not permit a full course in conflict management in this book. However, wise missionaries will study Scripture and take advantage of books and seminars to help gain skills in overcoming conflict. Cross-cultural issues make conflict resolution more complicated. Missionary families must understand their national counterparts personally and culturally if conflict is to be resolved.

The best way to manage stress generated by interpersonal conflict is to resolve the conflict. Chapter 8 "Reducing Stress by Resolving Conflict" will give you biblical insight into understanding and resolving conflict.

Cure or Escape? Harmful Ways of Handling Stress

Stressed people often resort to methods of managing their pain that cause more harm than good. Instead of curing the cause, they try to escape the symptom. Inevitably, they sink deeper into the morass of emotional and spiritual struggle. Families seeking to manage stress must carefully avoid some of these pitfalls.

Alcohol

You may have heard someone who has had a bad day say, "I need a drink." Unfortunately, alcohol has been used for many millennia by people trying to forget their problems. People who use alcohol to escape the stress of life end up having more stress. Consider Proverbs 23:29–35: "Who has woe? Who has sorrow? Who has contentions? Who has babbling? Who has wounds without cause? Who has redness of eyes? They that tarry long at the wine; they that go to seek mixed wine. Look not thou upon the wine when it is red, when it gives his color in the cup, when it moves itself aright. At the last it bites like a serpent, and stings like an adder. Your eyes shall behold strange women, and your heart shall utter perverse things. Yea, you shall be as he that lies down in the midst of the sea, or as he that lies upon the top of a mast. 'They have stricken me,' shalt thou say, 'and I was not sick; they have beaten me, and I felt it not: when shall I awake? I will seek it yet again.'"

God's litany of wisdom includes warnings against the dangers of alcohol:

- Wine is a mocker, strong drink is raging: and whosoever is deceived thereby is not wise (Proverbs 20:1).
- It is not for kings, O Lemuel, it is not for kings to drink wine; nor for princes strong drink: Lest they drink, and forget the law, and pervert the judgment of any of the afflicted (Proverbs 31:4–5).
- Woe unto them that are mighty to drink wine, and men of strength

to mingle strong drink:
Which justify the wicked for reward, and take away the righteousness of the righteous from him! (Isaiah 5:22–23).

- Woe unto them that rise up early in the morning, that they may follow strong drink; that continue until night, till wine inflame them! (Isaiah 5:11).

- But they also have erred through wine, and through strong drink are out of the way; the priest and the prophet have erred through strong drink, they are swallowed up of wine, they are out of the way through strong drink; they err in vision, they stumble in judgment. (Isaiah 28:7).

Hannah was a woman who experienced extreme stress. She was childless and wanted a child desperately. She could have responded to her situation in many ways, but listen to her testimony: "I am a woman of a sorrowful spirit: I have drunk neither wine nor strong drink, but have poured out my soul before the LORD" (1 Samuel 1:15). Instead of drowning her sorrows in liquor, she brought her problem to God!

Most missionaries experience no attraction to lapse into the use of alcohol. Their Christian commitment keeps them from using substances that hurt their witness and harm their prospects of winning the people to Jesus. At the same time, particularly if individuals had a history of alcohol use before salvation, the temptation to drown one's sorrows remains a real challenge, particularly in cultures where liquor is culturally acceptable.

Drugs

Some people use drugs to alter their moods. Marijuana, cocaine, crack (a form of cocaine), ecstasy, and others are designed to produce euphoric feelings, but, in the end, have disastrous results physically, emotionally, and spiritually. Amphetamines raise a person's alertness, but become highly addictive and can alter one's moods and may produce hallucinations. Amphetamines have been linked to heart attacks, strokes, and other causes of sudden death. Barbiturates are often used for sedation or anxiety problems but also produce sluggishness, poor judgment, and even death.

Few missionaries would resort to those drugs, but may be tempted to abuse prescription pharmaceuticals, including painkillers, sleep aids, and diet pills (which contain substances with amphetamine-like properties). Medications meant to elevate depressed persons can become substitutes for dealing with the spiritual issues behind the sorrowful moods. Legal and illegal pharmaceuticals are much more easily obtained in some countries where missionaries live and work, making addictions a genuine threat.

Sex

God created sex as a beautiful part of human life. Not only designed for procreation, sex was intended to express ultimate intimacy between a husband and wife. Emotional benefits likely outrank physical pleasure among the blessings of a loving sexual relationship. Scripture offers wise advice about the marriage covenant: ". . . rejoice with the wife of thy youth. Let her be as the loving hind and pleasant roe; let her breasts satisfy thee at all times; and be thou ravished always with her love" (Proverbs 5:15–19).

Unfortunately, some people abuse sex. When a woman senses her husband wants to have sex simply to relieve stress, she feels used. Instead of growing in affirmation and love, she devolves into an object for another's selfish satisfaction. Sex, rightly employed in a mutually giving act of affection, builds marriages up; wrongly exploited for self-gratification, it quickly tears down years of trust and tenderness. Sexual intimacy should be the most fulfilling expression of love and oneness between a husband and wife. It should not be reduced to a stress-management technique.

Shopping

With limited markets in many mission locations and limited money in most, shopping by missionary wives tends to relate to family needs. On the occasional furlough or trip to a conference city, the family may splurge for long-needed clothes, books, electronics, or other desires. Spending money on the few legitimate pleasures available on the field can be counted among the small blessings that plant smiles on the faces of a missionary family.

However, in some situations, shopping can be used as an outlet for the stress afflicted. When spending money becomes a temporary antidote for dissatisfaction, discouragement, or depression, it ceases being productive and often adds financial burdens to an already stressful environment. Neither is this problem limited to females. Men also misuse money during stress; only their purchases can be more costly and, in the case of escapism, more detrimental.

Escapism

Under stress, people look for an escape or, at least, a distraction. They often withdraw from relationships or interaction with family and friends. Instead of recognizing the source of the stress and dealing with it honestly and openly, they become vulnerable to temptations that promise a break.

The Internet has become one of the most common and dangerous vehicles for escape. While the Net provides a wonderful way for the family to maintain communication with distant friends and family, many ministry families have been torn apart by inappropriate and sinful misuse of the World Wide Web.

Missionaries and their families are not immune from becoming involved with unknown persons in an online chat room. Pornography also sits in cyberspace like a coiled adder, waiting to strike foolish folk who fool around with its hidden lures. Thinking no one will know, men and women (as well as teens, and even some children) regularly enter a world of fantasy and lust. They ignore godly wisdom: "Stolen waters are sweet, and bread eaten in secret is pleasant. But he knows not that the dead are there; and that her guests are in the depths of hell" (Proverbs 9:17–18).

Some ministers, wives, and teens find themselves addicted to sexual perversions. Left unchecked, their licentious appetites demand increasingly more lurid fantasies. All sorts of sexual sins lie at their door waiting to destroy them. Scripture warns young men (and by inference women as well): "When wisdom enters into your heart, and knowledge is pleasant unto your soul; Discretion shall preserve thee, understanding shall keep thee: To deliver thee from the way of the evil man, . . . Whose ways are crooked, . . . To deliver thee from the strange woman, even from the stranger which flatters with her words; Which forsakes the guide of her youth, and forgets the covenant of her God. For her house inclines unto death, and her paths unto the dead" (Proverbs 2:10–18).

Ministers caught in the Internet porn trap find themselves broken when caught by their spouse, or worse, their children. Through much counseling, sorrow, and repentance, they may receive forgiveness and reconciliation, but their families and their ministries suffer much pain in the process. Many other marriages have ended, with children, churches, family, and friends left in the wreckage.

Chapter Seven

Organizational Stress

While a few missionaries work totally independently, most operate within organizational systems. Even ministers who enlist their funding usually serve within an agency structure. Blessed is the missionary whose organization is well structured and managed with biblical principles and professional expertise. However, even the best mission board involves human beings who are subject to the same frailties and failures as the rest of us. Stress may arise due to differing visions and strategies, organizational structures, management of administrative personnel, conflicting views of policy interpretation or application, or personal conflict.

Vision and Strategy Development

God draws people to the mission field with a call and a vision. Each missionary responds to the inner prompting of the Holy Spirit and a vision of varying clarity about how he or she fits into God's plan. Paul had such a revelation during a dream-filled night in which he saw a man of Macedonia pleading for him to "Come over and help us" (Acts 16:6–10). Paul's original plan was to visit Asia. When the Holy Spirit vetoed that idea, Paul sought to visit Bithynia, but again the Spirit prevented him. At that point, God gave him a vision and a heart for Macedonia. If Paul had insisted on following his own plan and had not responded to God's calling, the church at Philippi might never have been born.

Vision is vital to every enterprise, especially for God's messengers. A familiar passage reminds us "where there is no vision, the people perish . . ." (Proverbs 29:18). Without a clear image of God's vision, people follow their individual desires, much like Israel before the days of kings when ". . . every man did that which was right in his own eyes" (Judges 17:6).

As long as people in an organization share a mutual vision and agree on how the vision should be accomplished, they can function effectively and cooperatively. However, given the nature of human beings, they generally come to a divergence of opinions at some point. Having varying ideas is not bad. In fact, only an unhealthy organization demands everyone go along in order to get along. Creativity emerges as people share their different approaches. As long as they maintain respect for one another and remain committed to the overall vision and purpose of the mission, they should find common ground on which to proceed.

Problems arise and stress is generated generally in at least two instances: (1) when workers begin to have personal visions and goals that do not support the organization's mission, or (2) when they develop plans at variance with the strategies of the agency or their coworkers.

The Problem of Human Vision

Sometimes ministers begin work with a vision for what they want and a plan for how they intend to accomplish their goals. While this approach sounds admirable, it can be part of the problem. Vision is never ours; true vision belongs to and comes from God.

Human vision tends to be self-centered in orientation, limited in scope, and presumptuous in nature. It is self-centered because it originates from the heart and mind of the individual rather than from the Holy Spirit. It is limited in scope because it can only encompass the human perspective rather than the ultimate intention of God. It is presumptuous in nature because it assumes God will provide whatever resources and power is needed to accomplish the goal, even if God did not initiate the plan.

Human vision creates conflict and stress because each individual can claim the right to follow his or her dream, regardless of what others' vision may involve. If two or more missionary units (families)

134

serve a common group of people, whose vision should determine what they will do? How they will go about it? In what areas can they cooperate? What results should they seek? Even if workers genuinely respect and care for one another, the pull of private visions can engender disagreement and disharmony.

Human vision can result in abuse of authority. Persons who occupy administrative positions over others may impose their ideas on people who are forced to accept the plan in order to keep their jobs. One mission leader called a meeting of workers under his supervision. He chastised them for a lack of progress in accomplishing various goals he had set for them based on his vision of the task. He told them they existed to help him succeed. Not only did he misunderstand their purpose (or his, for that matter), he failed to realize that, as someone once said: "Few people are less motivated than when in pursuit of someone else's goals." Just because a leader has the authority to impose his vision on others does not mean that he should.

The Benefits of God-Generated Vision

God-generated vision, on the other hand, brings people together. Harmony proceeds from having a shared purpose that is greater than oneself. When missionaries set aside personal desires and commit to seek God's will, they will eventually receive a clearer picture of His vision, drawing them together instead of pulling them apart.

While serving as director of the Missions Department for the Tennessee Baptist Convention, I had a leadership team composed of five persons with very different personalities. Each minister was passionate about helping churches reach people through his area of responsibility. This complex combination was ripe for conflict; however, the team was one of the most harmonious and productive groups I've ever known. One factor was a retreat in which we developed a common understanding of God's vision for our work. Our commitment to God's purpose motivated each of us to look past individual differences and work together for a common goal.

God-generated vision challenges His people. God showed Moses such an awesome vision that he could not take it in all at once. "And so terrible was the sight, that Moses said, I exceedingly fear and quake" (Hebrews 12:21). Paul put it this way, "Eye has not seen, nor ear heard,

135

neither has entered into the heart of man, the things which God has prepared for them that love him" (1 Corinthians 2:9). A group of leaders entered a retreat with the intention of learning new administrative skills. However, one presentation challenged the entire team to consider a radically different direction that would transform their strategy. After a lengthy meeting, they emerged convinced this vision was from the Lord. Committing to the new mandate, they restructured their plans for the next several years. The results were met with enthusiasm beyond their highest expectations.

> God-generated vision also guarantees divine provision for whatever is needed to accomplish God's purpose.

God-generated vision guarantees divine provision for whatever is needed to accomplish God's purpose. When Nehemiah heard about the conditions in Jerusalem, he immediately felt a tremendous burden for his people. He held the influential position of cupbearer to King Artaxerxes of Persia, but he was still a slave. If he had acted on his burden rather than waiting for God, he would have failed, and likely would have been executed. Instead, by patiently seeking God's vision and timing, he went forth with the king's permission, accompanied by a strong military guard, and possessing a letter from the king giving him access to the resources to fulfill the task. When we trust God to give us His vision, we can trust Him for everything needed for its fulfillment.

God-generated vision glorifies God, not human beings. When God gives people His vision, provides for the vision, and divinely accomplishes the vision, human instruments cannot claim credit even if God chooses to act through them. He alone is worthy of glory, honor, and praise.

Discovering God's Vision

Discovering God's vision takes time. Nehemiah waited four months before God said, "Go." God gives some visions in shorter time frames; others take much longer. God rarely is pictured being in a hurry. We need to put ourselves on His timetable and wait patiently on Him. Abraham tried to accomplish God's will through human effort, producing generations of war between his descendants. Only when he surrendered to God's vision did he receive the fruition of God's plan: "And so, after he had patiently endured, he obtained the promise" (Hebrews 6:15).

Discovering God's vision requires serious prayer and searching God's Word. God does not change His will to conform to our prayers. We pray to discern God's will and surrender ourselves to it. God invites us to share our desires and our dreams, our pain and our praise. Yet, in the end, the servant awaits the Master's pleasure and follows His instruction. Through serious prayer, we lay ourselves, our situations, our future—everything—before the Lord and allow Him to direct our hearts.

We also must study Scriptures to insure we are on solid ground in understanding God's plans. Too many people wander down the yellow brick road of their own desires thinking it is God's path, only to find themselves lost along the way because they failed to search God's Word. God will never say one thing in the Bible and something else to our hearts. Whatever we consider must be consistent with biblical principles.

Discovering God's vision requires faith. "By faith . . ." Those two small words preface some of the most powerful expressions of faith-based vision found in Scripture. Hebrews 11 has been called Faith's Hall of Fame because it recounts the mighty acts of Abraham and other patriarchs, as well as the unsung and unnamed heroes who suffered and died in faithful pursuit of God's vision. God-sized vision cannot be comprehended, much less embraced, without confident trust that God will accomplish whatever He initiates. "Faithful is he that calls you, who also will do it" (1 Thessalonians 5:24). God's vision does not require great abilities in His servants; it merely requires faith and faithfulness. If we believe God, we can be faithful to follow wherever He leads.

Organizational Structures

Stress may emanate from a mission agency's organizational structure. In some instances, discomfort may derive from poorly designed structure that becomes dysfunctional rather than aiding efficient and effective work. In other cases, an agency may change structures due to new directions of incoming leaders, new strategies, or new realities of the mission field itself.

Personality Incompatibility

Often, stress arises from a mismatch of personnel to structure. Some missionaries thrive by having a wide range of opportunities and freedom to pursue new ministries as they see fit. If the organization's structure has strict lines of authority and controlled decision making, these workers may sense growing frustration and subsequent stress. Marvin had served multiple terms on various fields, experiencing success in reaching new people and starting additional churches. He had an independent style by which he worked with local leaders to strategize and implement ministries quickly. When a new administrator initiated procedures that created a bottleneck, requiring all strategies and expenditures to be approved by him personally, Marvin grew increasingly dissatisfied. Instead of being able to work through the problem with his supervisor, Marvin's expression of displeasure created a growing rift in his agency, leading to his eventual departure from the work he loved.

On the other hand, missionaries who enjoy clearly defined work parameters and procedures may experience discomfort in an organization that values a more laissez faire style of administration. These personalities need set regulations and rules to create a safe, understandable environment. Bill worked well in a setting where expectations and processes were clearly delineated. Joining a missions' organization that enabled him to serve in his field of preference, his supervisors gave him great latitude in choosing methods and strategies but offered little support or direction. Bill experienced growing stress, as he could not get clear guidelines for his work.

Matching personalities and work environment helps reduce stressors within the organization's structure and aids enjoyable and productive labor. Additionally, mission agencies wishing to empower its workers in a less stressful environment, should give attention to management issues, logistical support, and financial accountability.

Management Issues

Most missionaries enjoy good relations through the various administrative strata, primarily because of their mutual commitments to the Lord and their common mission. Some missionaries work in a relatively independent structure, primarily due to their isolation from central offices. Consequently, management issues primarily relate to submitting reports of activities and results, occasional meetings at mission hubs, and communication via email or Skype. Stress relating to management may be minimized by distance but remains a challenge at times. Typical problems include incompatibility between regional leaders and field missionaries related to strategies or style of implementation, personalities, logistical support, and financial accountability.

Strategy development generally involves collaboration between regional leaders and the various missionaries related to a specific field. In the case of larger agencies, senior leaders direct a general strategy while regional leaders develop tactical applications related to their assigned people groups. Implementation of the strategy usually is left to the discretion of the local missionaries. At each level, conflict is possible. International directors may not understand nuances of local situations, issuing directives for a macrostrategy that conflicts with on-the-ground realities. Conversely, individual missionaries may not see the forest for the trees; their focus on micro-strategies may limit their perspective of the larger picture. Each scenario creates tension between leaders. Collaboration at all levels of leadership, commitment to mutual respect, and willingness to be flexible are keys to minimizing organizational stress.

Logistical support affects not only the effectiveness of ministries, but the security of the missionaries and their families. Most ministers depend on their agency structures to provide support for their ministries, including provisions of funds, legal and administrative assistance, and coordination with other missionaries and local leaders. Additionally, their families rely on area administrators for housing, transportation, visa requirements, language education, and other basic necessities. When problems emerge with the flow of support, the missionary and his family experience understandable distress. Not only is his ministry hindered, but his family also feels threatened. Finding enough funds for all the needs and opportunities on any mission field is daunting. Assigning limited resources among competing good causes stress for mission administrators as well as field workers.

Logistical complications may result from internal or external sources. Internal problems may include faulty communication, lack of competency, or conflicting priorities. External issues may involve government interference, unforeseen financial shortfalls, transportation strikes, or other problems.

Overcoming logistically related stress requires patience and cooperation on all sides.

Financial accountability provides another area for potential stress. Missionaries must be accountable for financial resources whether they are employed by an agency or use deputation to raise funds for family and ministry needs. Paperwork—from budgets to requisitions to reimbursements—can be complicated and time consuming. Few people enjoy taking time from field work to handle administrative forms. If administrators, office workers, or missionaries cannot manage necessary bookkeeping with mutual cooperation, everyone may experience anxiety whenever quarterly reports are due.

Personnel Administration

Selection. How does an agency turn down someone who wants to be a missionary? The missionary family has responded to what they believe to be God's call and is willing to give up the comfort of familiar surroundings to follow God's leading to reach unchurched people domestically or internationally. They are sincere and committed. How do you say no to that kind of faith?

Missions agencies have a responsibility not only to the people to whom the missionary will go but to the missionary family to conduct an effective selection process. Some people have a sincere belief in their call but have other issues, making service problematic. Theological discussions help determine doctrinal compatibility between agencies and laborers. Psychological reviews may reveal unresolved personal problems that might impact the workers, especially when they enter the stress of the mission field. Financial assessments measure whether a family carries debt that would hinder their work, as well as whether they have demonstrated wisdom in personal financial decisions.

In some cases, issues arise in the interview and testing process that preclude someone from service. Understandably, if an agency declines an application, disappointment, discouragement, and dissension linger long after the decisions are made. Discussing the personnel for the Second Missionary Journey, Paul and Barnabus engaged in an intractable conflict over whether John Mark should be part of the team. Paul adamantly refused on the basis that Mark had left the company during their previous trip. Barnabus insisted Mark be given a second chance.

Some people assume that Mark departed because of the hardships and persecution. However, study of the scriptural account indicates the group had not experienced hardships up to that point. Acts 13 reveals a key to understanding the issue. When the first missionary journey began, the order of authority was Barnabus and Saul. However, after Saul's miraculous handling of Elymas the sorcerer, the group became known as "Paul and his company" (v. 13). In the wake of Barnabus losing his position of leadership to Paul, John Mark left the group and returned to Jerusalem. Barnabus, ever the encourager, did not seem to object to Paul's ascendency. However, Mark may have been offended and had chosen to leave the group. Paul and Barnabus split company rather than come up with an acceptable solution. Each chose a partner and went separate ways.

The selection process intends to provide a beneficial alignment of personnel to assignment. Whether the candidates are accepted or declined, the process itself is stressful. Prior preparation of candidates for the process itself can reduce anxiety and enable the entire family to enjoy a positive experience.

Orientation and Training. Would-be missionaries who launch their families onto a mission field without proper orientation and training set themselves, their wives, and their children up for intense stress and possible failure. Even independent missionaries benefit from some degree of preparation before going to the field. Workers affiliated with a formal agency have the benefit of proven training modules to prepare them and their families for their new lives.

Culture and language: Many missionaries have already had some connection with their prospective places of service. Increasingly large numbers of career workers will have already served on short-term volunteer teams, usually in the location where they are placed. Still, visiting temporarily does not begin to reveal the intricacies of culture and language. While the adults may have had a wonderful experience visiting this new land, their children may be seeing it for the first time. The prospect of the unknown can be frightening.

On the other hand, when MKs face their futures with faith in their parents and in God, they can be inspirational. Our grandson was eight years old when his family moved to Australia. After a couple of months, he told his mother, "Isn't God good to have given us a nice place to live? I thought we'd be living on a dirt floor with a rug over it." He was willing to go even though his image of their future lifestyle was much more primitive than it turned out to be. His commitment to God's call for his family was inspirational to us all.

Solid orientation can alleviate fears and prepare all members of the family to know what to expect and how to handle the challenges of a new life. Yet, even the training itself can be stressful. Learning about different customs, foods, insects, snakes, possible dangers, and even the prospect of having to replace appliances with machines that work on different electrical voltage— all can provoke the imagination and produce various levels of anxiety.

Working through the different issues is part of the orientation process. As families talk and pray through their concerns, they will gradually come to peace and, even, excitement about the prospects ahead.

Methodologies and strategies: Another part of orientation and training involves methodologies and strategies to help missionaries accomplish their tasks. Most mission fields have had workers serving over extended periods of time. They have learned what succeeds and what does not. The experiences of many missionaries go into the training experiences for new workers. Having a starting place helps reduce the stress of first-time missionaries. The more they know ahead of beginning the work, the more confident they are as they commence their work.

In those few situations where new missionaries are the first to enter a particular field, the mission agency generally has sent other field personnel to scout out the land. They have studied the worldviews of the people group, their customs and beliefs, and have developed preliminary strategies and methods designed to reach that particular culture. While the missionaries likely will develop their own strategies after having some time on the field, having a starting place is better than having to reinvent the wheel!

Spiritual preparation: Jesus reminds us that we can do nothing of ourselves. Only as we abide in Him can we expect to bear fruit (John 15:5). Much of an agency's orientation program involves spiritual preparation.

Personal counsel, public worship, and group training—as individuals and as families—help potential workers begin their new work with a strong sense of communion with Christ.

In many places, the family may not have an established church with which to worship and fellowship. That's why they are missionaries—starting new work where there is none. They have to be prepared to nourish each other spiritually. Discovering the joys of family worship enables the missionary family to be satisfied and grow spiritually without the benefit of other believers.

Crisis management: Increasingly, missionaries serve in places that hold genuine physical dangers. In some cases, religious animosity against Christians in general and American missionaries, specifically, puts them at risk. In other locations, bandits have kidnapped individuals or whole families for ransom. Mission agencies include strong instruction on how to avoid dangerous situations and what to do if a crisis does occur.

In being prepared to handle hazardous incidents, missionaries may experience significant anxiety. The knowledge that they or their children might be in danger can be intimidating. The better trained the entire family can be, the less stress they will experience. Still, only their faith in God and His protective hand will suffice to give them the emotional peace necessary to fulfill their calling in difficult locations.

Supervision. Supervision on the mission field takes many different forms. Since many workers live at some distance from their supervisors, daily oversight may be limited. In some cases, a freer and more flexible working relationship can empower the missionary to follow his own direction as he develops his ministry. On the other hand, some workers benefit from more hands-on guidance.

Supervision should not be seen as heavy-handed micromanagement in a top-down authority structure. Supervision at its best involves a structure designed to help every missionary reach full potential. The relationship between supervisors and field personnel must be characterized by mutual respect, sincere cooperation, and an overarching commitment to the cause of Christ, not some personal agenda.

The goal of any supervisory meeting should be to help and facilitate both the work and the workers. Some levels of tension will arise as correction has to be initiated, new strategies or procedures redefined, or some other type of change becomes necessary. Good supervision allows both sides to communicate openly and honestly about concerns, needs, and problems. Stress can be reduced and managed if everyone involved maintains servant hearts and godly attitudes with the intent to glorify Christ in all things.

Evaluation. One of the most disliked aspects of personnel management is evaluation. Supervisors and workers alike tend to dislike those annual reviews that seem to put an element of "pass-fail" to what should be spiritual work. One of the underlying causes of such attitudes is a misunderstanding of what evaluation should be and how it should occur.

Myron Rush has one of the most effective approaches to evaluation in his book, *Management: A Biblical Approach*. Rush argues that evaluation should be a two-way street. Supervisors not only give workers their assessment of what has gone well and not so well, but they also encourage workers to share what they need from the supervisors in order to succeed.[1]

Rush also rightly observes that the old end-of-the-year review is nearly worthless. Part of the year may have been successful and part not so successful. Which part will be considered in the evaluation? In addition, when evaluation does not occur until the end of the year, the worker and supervisor have no chance to adjust and improve during the year. Rush advocates a quarterly formal evaluation accompanied by ongoing informal discussions in between meetings.[2]

When missionaries and their supervisors enjoy reciprocated respect and cultivate a personal as well as professional relationship, both can reduce their anxiety about evaluations and supervision in general. Instead of dreading evaluations, they can eagerly anticipate opportunities to achieve mutually beneficial encouragement and achievement.

Discipline and Reward. An inevitable aspect of evaluation involves discipline and reward. No one enjoys being disciplined, yet if evaluation (formal or informal) reveals the need for correction, good supervisors do what is best—not only for the organization but for the missionary. To allow someone to continue on the wrong direction does not help the worker improve, nor does it honor the responsibility the mission has to the unreached people to whom the missionary ministers.

When missionaries receive correction with a positive attitude, they can adjust and become more effective in their work. On the other hand, if the problem lies not only in competence, but with their basic character, the nature and extent of discipline may involve more serious consequences. In any case, both the supervisor exercising discipline and the worker receiving it experience stress. However, if each party commits to honoring God and seeks the best for His people, everyone can work through the process satisfactorily.

While the stress of discipline is obvious, rewarding progress can offer its own subtle stress. Reward may involve simple recognition for work well done, an increase in compensation, promotion within the organization, or even assignment to a more desired venue for service. Such benefits sound wonderful, and they are. So where does the stress lie? Some rewards, such as promotion or reassignment, involve significant change, which itself is stressful.

In a few cases, people are very effective at one level, but are not as competent at a higher position. One example is a field worker who was successful as a lone church planter among the ethnic group to which he belonged. Promoted several levels with a large staff to manage, he found himself needing a totally different skill set for which he was not prepared.

Even if a person succeeds in a new position, he has to adjust the way he relates to people. Coworkers who have been peers find themselves under their friend's supervision. Some may react with jealousy and resist the new administrator's leadership. Others may expect favored status with the boss based on past relationships. Both attitudes can present problems, which is why promotions often involve relocation to a different location with new colleagues.

Still, in most situations, everyone involved shares mutual commitments to the Lord and His mission, motivating them to make either discipline or reward work to the honor of God and the good of His people.

Managing Volunteers

Over the past twenty years, a major shift in missiological strategy has changed the landscape of many mission fields. Historically, most mission efforts were led by career missionaries who invested their lives in a distant land or who moved to a pioneer area of North America to begin a new church. While thousands of missionaries still provide the foundation of mission work, they have been joined by tens of thousands of volunteers. Most volunteers limit their work to short-term trips of a few weeks; however, some give two years or more to a specific people group.

Long-term volunteers include college students who spend a summer on the field or graduates who give two years filling vital needs. Older volunteers are finding a second career investing their professional skills and knowledge on a mission field. Most volunteers work in close support of a career missionary, while a few may link with indigenous ministers.

How do you manage people who are not being paid? A friend who was responsible for hundreds of volunteer workers at a major health-care system developed several effective principles. My application of her principles produced these recommendations:

- Establish a position, including job description, for each need—just as with paid workers.
- Interview candidates, judging their suitability for the specific positions—just as with paid workers.
- Supervise volunteers with expectation of a reasonable level of effectiveness and proper attitudes—just as with paid workers.
- Evaluate volunteers and give correction or reward based on results—just as with paid workers.
- Discipline volunteers, including dismissal if necessary—just as with paid workers.

In other words, by treating volunteers the same as paid workers, they feel more respected and are motivated to perform at superior levels.

However positive the relationships may be, handling volunteers still produces various levels of stress for the career missionary supervisor as well as the volunteers. The normal supervisory issues affect everyone involved. Moreover, additional elements complicate the process. Volunteers will not be as trained either theologically or in mission methodology. They generally lack language proficiency and need the provision of a translator. The career missionary may have to take time away from regular responsibilities to provide logistics, including transportation and housing, as well as personal support.

When multiple volunteers are involved, such as with short-term mission trips, the missionary may have to suspend normal work to handle the myriad needs of a larger group. Short-term groups can provide valuable assistance for the career worker, but also require significant investment of time. Handling all the arrangements for housing, transportation, and translation for the group is only part of the work. The missionary also must coordinate with indigenous ministers and churches with whom the volunteers will work. In addition, short-term groups tend to expect at least part of their trip to involve normal tourist activities, further complicating the missionary's schedule.

While long-term volunteers generally undergo training and orientation, short-term workers have limited preparation at best. Consequently, they may make cultural or other mistakes, usually unintentionally, with the potentially damaging consequences for the career workers and their ongoing ministry. Sometimes, the missionary must invest significant time rebuilding relationships with indigenous people if a volunteer does or says something offensive. Both sides of this partnership can have a more stress-free experience if they take positive steps, such as the following:

- Establish the specific purpose of the short-term mission trip well in advance. The mission will go much smoother if each party understands about why people are going and what they will be doing.
- Establish some reasonable level of expectations regarding qualification of short-term volunteers, including spiritual maturity and physical abilities to handle strenuous or unhygienic conditions if applicable.
- Require advance training of all volunteers, including mission-specific information, cultural orientation, and spiritual preparation.

- Prepare indigenous workers for the team—not merely the logistics, but a cultural orientation so they might know what to expect from relatively untrained foreign visitors.
- Involve everyone—volunteers, missionaries, and indigenous personnel—in prayer support for the mission before, during, and after the trip.
- Insure that all participants—missionaries and volunteers—plan out logistical issues in advance, including specific financial details. One of the most consistent causes of conflict regarding short-term trips involves unexpected expenses or major changes in the nature of the work.
- Communicate openly and honestly before, during, and after the trip. When people talk with one another about expectations, problems, and concerns, they usually find ways to reconcile issues before they explode into conflict.
- Evaluate each level of preparation and execution. Don't wait until after the trip is over. Before the group goes home, have a round-table discussion about what has gone well and what could be improved. Reach an agreement about what will be done differently in the future and offer thanks for each person's efforts during the mission.
- Watch the tapes. Review the results of the mission after it is all over and make adjustments for future mission groups accordingly.

The stress for everyone involved in volunteer missions can be significant. Still, with Christian commitment to one another and mutual desire for the advancement of God's kingdom in the mission setting, volunteers and career missionaries can work through the challenges successfully.

CHAPTER EIGHT

Reducing Stress by Resolving Conflict

"As much as it lies within you, live peaceably with all men"
(Romans 12:18).

Conflict produces more stress than most other issues in our lives. No one likes conflict. Most people prefer positive, mutually encouraging relationships, but conflict tends to interrupt our lives in spite of our best intentions. Conflict may center on task issues—what to do and how to do it. Conflict also arises from interactions between various personality types.

The best way to resolve conflict is to avoid it. By demonstrating the fruit of the Spirit in all relationships, we are more likely to provoke positive responses. Generally, people will react well if we are loving instead of hateful, joyful rather than sour, peaceful rather than combative, patient rather than short tempered, gentle rather than rough, good rather than evil, faithful rather than undependable, meek rather than arrogant, and temperate rather than self-indulgent (Galatians 5:16–23).

Scripture offers wise insight for good, stress-free relationships. Consider several examples from the book of Proverbs:

- Withhold not good from them to whom it is due (Proverbs 3:27).
- Devise not evil against your neighbor (Proverbs 3:29).
- Put away from you a forward mouth, and perverse lips

put far from you (Proverbs 4:24).

- Hatred stirs up strife: but love covers all sins (Proverbs 10:12).
- The merciful man does good to his own soul: but he that is cruel troubles his own flesh (Proverbs 11:17).
- Deceit is in the heart of them that imagine evil: but to the counselors of peace is joy (Proverbs 12:20).
- Lying lips are abomination to the LORD: but they that deal truly are his delight (Proverbs 12:22),
- He that is slow to wrath is of great understanding: but he that is hasty of spirit exalts folly (Proverbs 14:29).
- The beginning of strife is as when one lets out water: therefore leave off contention, before it is meddled with (Proverbs 17:14).
- A man that hath friends must show himself friendly: and there is a friend that sticks closer than a brother (Proverbs 18:24).
- Go not forth hastily to strive, lest you know not what to do in the end, when your neighbor puts you to shame. Debate your cause with your neighbor himself; and discover not a secret to another: Lest he that hears it puts you to shame. . . . (Proverbs 25:8–10).
- Where no wood is, there the fire goes out: so where there is no talebearer, the strife ceases (Proverbs 26:20).
- A lying tongue hates those that are afflicted by it; and a flattering mouth works ruin (Proverbs 26:28).
- A man's pride shall bring him low: but honor shall uphold the humble in spirit (Proverbs 29:23).

If we incorporate spiritual wisdom into our relationships, we can avoid much sorrow caused by conflict. Avoiding attitudes and actions that hurt others stops the fire before it starts. At the same time, we should cultivate those behaviors that build up the relationship by benefiting other people. As we follow the model our Savior gave in His life and in His teaching, we can offer the basis for love rather than conflict.

The Ministry of Reconciliation

"And all things are of God, who has reconciled us to himself by Jesus Christ, and has given to us the ministry of reconciliation; To wit, that God was in Christ, reconciling the world unto Himself, not imputing their trespasses unto them; and has committed unto us the word of reconciliation. Now then we are ambassadors for Christ, as though God did beseech you by us: we pray you in Christ's stead, be reconciled to God" (2 Corinthians 5:18–20).

God has given us the ministry and word of reconciliation. Believers are the recipients of His gracious work of reconciliation, bringing us into a right relationship with Him through Jesus. As such, we have received a ministry of reconciliation. The foundation of the ministry of reconciliation is the word of reconciliation: ". . . that God was in Christ, reconciling the world unto Himself . . ." (2 Corinthians 5:19). The basis by which we can help people resolve interpersonal conflict is God's atoning work in Christ.

Reconciliation begins with Christ, then one another. Only Jesus can bring true peace within one's heart and between His people (John 14:27). Mediators who work with believers should begin by talking about their relationship with Christ. Jesus in one person cannot be in conflict with Jesus within another person. Where conflict exists, one or more of the parties have stepped away from a committed, submitted relationship to the Lord. Bringing each person closer to Christ, by nature, results in their coming closer to one another. Jesus Himself provides the strongest common ground for people to experience reconciliation. ". . . as though God did beseech you by us: we pray you in Christ's stead, be reconciled to God" (2 Corinthians 5:20).

Being peacemakers identifies us as children of God. Jesus is the Prince of Peace (Isaiah 9:6). We show ourselves to be His children and experience His blessing when we engage in making peace (Matthew 5:9). Disliking conflict, we may shy away from intervening into other people's conflicts, but such is the ministry He has given us. Much more, when we are part of the conflict, we cannot escape our responsibility to join Jesus in the ministry of peacemaking.

When conflict happens despite the best efforts, what can we do to resolve the disagreement and, in doing so, reduce the stress? Proverbs 20:3 reminds us: "It is honorable for a man to resolve a dispute, but any fool can get himself into a quarrel." So, what should you do if you find yourself in conflict?

Steps to Resolving Interpersonal Conflict

1. Honestly examine yourself.

Jesus said we should examine our hearts before we attempt to correct someone else: "And why do you behold the speck that is in thy brother's eye, but perceive not the beam that is in your own eye? Either how can you say to your brother, 'Brother, let me pull out the speck that is in your eye,' when you do not see the beam that is in your own eye? You hypocrite, cast out first the beam out of your own eye, and then you will see clearly to pull out the speck that is in your brother's eye" (Luke 6:41–42).

Honestly ask yourself if you are at fault in some way. Have you said or done something to provoke the dispute? Have you exhibited an attitude that offended the other person? Do you really love this person and want the best for him/her?

2. Lovingly understand the other person(s).

Do you understand what problems they may be dealing with at work, in the home, or personally? It may be that the conflict you are experiencing is actually fallout from conflict or difficulties in other places, producing stress that carries over into other relationships.

Could you be experiencing a cross-personality conflict? As mentioned earlier, various personality types have difficulty understanding and relating to certain other types. Have you considered that each of you has approached an issue from your particular personality perspectives, and you really need each other to gain a more complete understanding of the situation?

Have you wondered what this person wants from you and whether such expectations are legitimate? Does this person think you have not lived up to a perceived agreement? Or vice versa? What does this person really need from you?

Have you prayed about where this person is in relationship with the Lord? People who are not right with God will not be right with people. On the other hand, "When a man's ways please the LORD, he makes even his enemies to be at peace with him" (Proverbs 16:7).

3. Do not be quick to judge.

Take time to listen and understand. Too often, we tend to jump to judgment. Instead of wisely listening to all sides to a dispute, we offer quick fixes that usually do more harm than good. "He who answers a matter before he hears it, It is folly and shame to him" (Proverbs 18:13). Peace makers invest sufficient time to understand what is actually going on before trying to solve the problem.

Recognize your own liability. Don't be quick to judge because we all will be judged. "But why do you judge your brother? or why do you set at naught your brother? for we shall all stand before the judgment seat of Christ" (Romans 14:10).

Be fair. If we expect others to do what is right, we must be fair in handling all conflicts. We, too, have a Judge who will utilize whatever standard of judgment we have employed with others. "Judge not, that you be not judged. For with what judgment you judge, you shall be judged: and with what standard you measure, it shall be measured to you again" (Matthew 7:1–2).

Employ wise discernment. Avoiding being judgmental does not mean we cannot be discerning. Maintaining order in the body of Christ requires us to use godly wisdom in determining the truth when fellow believers have disagreements. "Dare any of you, having a matter against another, go to law before the unjust, and not before the saints? Do ye not know that the saints shall judge the world? and if the world shall be judged by you, are ye unworthy to judge the smallest matters? Know ye not that we shall judge angels? how much more things that pertain to this life?" (1 Corinthians 6:1–3).

Avoid a spirit of condemnation. Attitudes can make or break conflict resolution. If we approach others with a spirit of condemnation, we not only will fail to achieve reconciliation, but we also put ourselves in danger of judgment and condemnation. "Judge not, and you shall not be judged: condemn not, and you shall not be condemned: forgive, and you shall be forgiven" (Luke 6:37).

4. Wisely discern the real issues behind the conflict.

Identify evidence of sin at the root of conflict. "From whence come wars and fighting among you? Come they not hence, even of your lusts that war in your members?" (James 4:1). Too often, people in conflict focus on assigning blame instead of resolving the problem. Everyone involved in a problem should humbly search their hearts to discern personal responsibility for sinful desires at the root of the fight. If the other person is at fault, love him/her enough to deal with the issue in a humble manner (Galatians 6:1).

Is one of the parties to the conflict fearful of losing face (self-esteem)? I spoke with one minister who had become engaged in a terrible conflict with a church leader. The issue seemed so trivial I asked why he had not merely yielded for the sake of the relationship. He answered that he felt he would lose his place of leadership if he let the other person win. He would rather risk ruining a relationship and damaging the peace of the congregation than appear not to be in control. Granted, some situations require courageous stands against evil. However, this situation came down to one matter—pride.

Some disagreements relate to generational perceptions and values. Various age groups approach decisions differently. The environmental influences of their generations often develop values that differ greatly from other age groups. For example, the builder generation (older people, many of whom experienced the Great Depression) are fearful of debt and tend to be very frugal. The baby boomers grew up on credit and were only interested in whether they can make the payments. When a ministry decision relates to financial questions, these two generations will approach solutions from very different perspectives.

Past experiences may shape a person's attitude. The person in conflict with you may see in you some aspect of another person who offended them in the past. One leader sought to change the church's procedures to eliminate much of the pastor's authority. When asked why he was so determined to make these drastic, conflict-causing changes, the leader related how a previous pastor had done something the layman felt was dishonest. He did not trust any pastor. In such cases, you have to help people open up about previous conflicts, show them you are not that person and this is not the same situation, and aid their coming to peace with their past so they might be at peace with their present.

Pain also influences people's reactions to situations and other people that may have nothing to do with the pain. One layman and his pastor experienced constant conflict in committee meetings. It seemed that no matter what the pastor did or said, the lay leader took the opposite position, often using strong emotion to insist on his point. Later, the pastor discovered that the layman was experiencing several painful situations. His employer was downsizing, creating fear he may lose his job. His son had become very rebellious and started using drugs. He was also suffering from a health problem that potentially could become life threatening. His personal pain did not excuse his behavior at church, but understanding it enabled the pastor to minister to the man with love and greater understanding.

Some conflicts relate to task issues, while other problems are personal. Understand whether the disagreement is over how to accomplish a particular task or if the conflict has taken on a personal nature. People-oriented conflict is much more difficult to resolve and requires different approaches.

5. Try to limit the number of persons involved in the matter.

Scripture advises anyone involved in conflict to approach the other person privately. "Moreover if your brother shall trespass against you, go and tell him his fault between you and him alone: if he shall hear you, you have gained your brother" (Matthew 18:15). The more people that are involved, the more difficult the resolution becomes. Pride rises. Sides are drawn. Advice starts flying from everyone at once, often without much wisdom, prayer, or seeking of Scriptural guidance. Peer pressure and the herd mentality are very real, creating an intractable situation.

6. Remember what is at stake.

Who wins or loses is not as important as the honor and glory of God. When Christians fight, they dishonor the name of the One they claim as Lord. Jesus said, "By this shall all men know that you are my disciples, if you have love one for another" (John 13:35). In dealing with disagreements, both parties need to consider what God gets from the way they approach the problem and one another.

In addition, lost people often judge Christ on the basis of Christians' behavior. Does the community know you as people who love one another or as persons who cannot even be in right relationship with members of your own church? In a missions setting, especially, the reputation of the missionaries (between one another and within families) may determine the responsiveness of the people group with whom they are working.

In Shantung Province, China (currently called Shandong Province), prior to the Maoist revolution, a group of missionaries had labored for years with little fruit. A small Lutheran missionary lady, Marie Monsoon, entered the community and began asking each person she met: "Are you born again? Are you filled with the Spirit?" At first, other missionaries were offended at her questions. Then, one by one, they began to come under conviction for their attitudes toward one another. Missionaries from different denominational backgrounds, and even those within the same mission teams, had been unloving, envious, and, in some cases, hostile to each other. As God's Spirit humbled them, they began apologizing to each other and became reconciled to God and to one another. A great movement of God began with those missionaries, known today as the Shantung Revival.[1] It swept first through the missionaries and then through the people of the land. Many came to Christ. Perhaps the only hindrance to evangelism and revival in some mission points today lies in the hearts and relationships of God's workers.

7. Understand your part in the matter.

Are you a participant or a peacemaker? Are you involved in the conflict or can you approach a problem as a third party whose only partiality is to the honor of God? If you are party to the problem, you may need to be humble enough to seek a mediator to help resolve the situation. Jesus taught that if one cannot resolve an issue privately, then ". . . take with you one or two more, that in the mouth of two or three witnesses every word may be established" (Matthew 18:16). The witnesses are not simply people who will take one side against the other. Rather, they are able to impartially view both points of view and may be able to mediate a resolution. In any case, they can testify to what is actually said and done between the conflicted parties.

Avoid being drawn into someone else's fight. Some people will share a problem with you, expecting you to set the other person straight. Their battle becomes yours and they often retire to the sidelines without responsibility for resolution or results, leaving you to suffer the scars that ensue. On the other hand, if you refuse to play their game, they may begin to perceive you as part of the problem and seek other people to take up their cause, often against you!

Realize that good shepherds protect the flock, even from themselves. Unfortunately, sheep bite! The shepherd who intervenes in conflict may discover painfully that some people will stop fighting each other long enough to attack you before going back to their battle. Still, good shepherds are willing to lay down their lives for the sheep. They do what is necessary to bring the sheep back to the Great Shepherd, Jesus, who is the Prince of Peace. In doing so, they may hear His voice: "Blessed are the peacemakers: for they shall be called the children of God" (Matthew 5:9).

8. Take the initiative to resolve the conflict, regardless of who is at fault.

People in conflict may be fearful of approaching others with whom they have conflict. Scripture reminds us that perfect love casts out fear. "There is no fear in love; but perfect love casts out fear: because fear hath torment. He that fears is not made perfect in love" (1 John 4:18). Prayerfully ask God to love the other person(s) through you. When you come to the point of caring more for the other person than for your own pride or position, you are ready to initiate reconciliation and resolution.

Most people are willing to resolve conflict if the other person admits wrongdoing and asks forgiveness. Scripture does not give us the luxury of placing the responsibility for action on others. Regardless of who is at fault, we have the responsibility to go to the other person and initiate reconciliation.

If you have harmed the other person, humbly admit the wrongdoing and ask for forgiveness. Confession may be difficult, particularly if the other party has also hurt you. Still, your responsibility is not what the other person may or may not do. You can only obey God's commandment for your actions. "Therefore if you bring your gift to the altar, and there remember that your brother has anything against you; Leave your gift before the altar, and go your way; first be reconciled to your brother, and then come and offer your gift" (Matthew 5:23–24).

Don't wait until the person at fault comes to you. I was sharing with a godly friend about a Christian leader who had wronged me. I said, "If he would just come and admit his wrong, we could be reconciled." My friend replied, "You have just identified the spiritual one in this problem." He pointed out Galatians 6:1. "Brothers, if a man be overtaken in a fault, you which are spiritual, restore such an one in the spirit of meekness; considering yourself, lest you also be tempted" (Galatians 6:1). I knew immediately that I had to call the other person and initiate reconciliation.

9. Pray together.

Put the matter in God's hand and seek to know the mind of Christ. It is hard to be angry with someone as you pray with them. During my tenure as state missions director, we received many requests from church planters for grants to purchase land. During the inspection of one proposed property, I saw immediately the location was totally unsuitable for a church. No amount of reasoning would convince the church leaders that they should look elsewhere. Instead of pursuing a discussion that was quickly degenerating into conflict, we knelt on the muddy ground and prayed earnestly for God's leadership. Each person became convinced this was not the right place for the church. A year later, the pastor, who was not at the church when the location was chosen, saw me at a meeting and expressed strong gratitude for the resolution that enabled the church to build in a different, perfectly placed location without conflict.

10. Act.

Do not delay. Several practical reasons suggest you should take action as soon as the conflict becomes known:

- As time goes by, anger turns to bitterness, making resolution much more difficult.
- When caught early, most adversaries have not reached intractable positions.
- If allowed to go unchecked, conflict draws other people like flies to trash, creating a much more complex situation.
- Conflict is like an infection; it rarely heals itself but only gets worse.

Scripture also commands believers to move quickly to resolve disagreements:

- "Agree with your adversary quickly, while you are in the way with him; lest at any time the adversary delivers you to the judge, and the judge delivers you to the officer, and you are cast into prison" (Matthew 5:25). Whether the other person is at fault, or we are wrong, the principle remains—work quickly to resolve the issue. Delayed reconciliation leads to escalation of the conflict, always causing more harm than the original problem.
- "Be ye angry, and sin not: let not the sun go down upon your wrath: Neither give place to the devil" (Ephesians 4:26–27). Delaying reconciliation prevents anger from being resolved. Allowed to go on unchecked, anger develops into bitterness. When we refuse to deal with our anger, we give the devil a platform within our hearts to attack our relationship with God and other people.

11. Remain calm and speak gently.

"A soft answer turns away wrath: but grievous words stir up anger" (Proverbs 15:1). Replacing anger with godly, Spirit-generated love allows you to respond to others with a humble heart. Instead of speaking with raised voice and strident spirit, you can speak in such a manner as to reduce the other person's anger. Once a fellow minister angrily approached me about a matter. He stood up, raised his voice, and gestured threateningly. Having grown up constantly fighting, my base nature was to also stand and respond in kind. However, God gave grace, enabling me to remain seated, speaking in a low voice. The louder he got, the softer I spoke—not in fear but following the Spirit's leading. Soon, the man realized his anger was inappropriate. He sat down, lowered his voice, and allowed us to enter a genuine discussion of the issue. Reconciliation ended with both of us praying, thanking God for His grace.

12. Lovingly rebuke wrongdoing.

Going to other people does not mean you ignore their wrongdoing. "Take heed to yourselves: If thy brother trespass against thee, rebuke him; and if he repent, forgive him" (Luke 17:3). The word that is translated *rebuke* is the Greek word *epitimaō*. The sense of the passage does not suggest a harsh accusation, but a firm admonishment. You may express strong disapproval, yet do so in a loving and gentle manner, remembering your own shortcomings (Galatians 6:1).

13. Beware of holding grudges.

Some personalities get mad easily, but get over anger quickly. Others take time to boil over, yet retain anger. Unfortunately, too many people blame their personality type for their unwillingness to deal with their lack of willingness to reconcile. In addition, many people justify their bitterness by pointing out others' wrongdoing.

Believers have no excuse. We are more than the sum of our personalities because the Holy Spirit lives within us. We are responsible to submit to the Scriptural admonition: "Grudge not one against another, brethren, lest you be condemned: behold, the judge stands before the door" (James 5:9).

14 Forgive and to ask forgiveness.

Scripture admonishes us to rebuke offenders, but equally commands us to forgive. (Luke 17:3) Interestingly, many people in ministry spend much of their teaching ministry talking about forgiveness, but in personal practice are among the most reluctant to forgive. Throughout the New Testament, believers are admonished to forgive. Consider these passages:

- "Forbearing one another, and forgiving one another, if any man has a quarrel against any: even as Christ forgave you, so also do you" (Colossians 3:13). Christ has forgiven us such heinous sins that only His blood on the cross could make atonement. If He has forgiven us for such great wrongs, how can we refuse to forgive others? "And be kind one to another, tenderhearted, forgiving one another, even as God for Christ's sake hath forgiven you" (Ephesians 4:32).

- Sometimes we forgive, only to have the other person continue to harm us. At what point do we stop "turning the other cheek?" Jesus gives us the answer through His lesson to Peter: "Then came Peter to him, and said, Lord, how often shall my brother sin against me, and I forgive him? Till seven times? Jesus said unto him, I say not unto you, Until seven times: but, Until seventy times seven" (Matthew 18:21–22). Jesus then told a parable of a man who owed much and was forgiven, only to be unforgiving toward a fellow servant who owed him a small amount. When other servants told the king, the unforgiving man was thrown into prison and his forgiven debt reissued. Jesus warned His followers: "So likewise shall my heavenly Father do also unto you, if you from your hearts forgive not everyone his brother their trespasses" (Matthew 18:35). The key phrase is "from the heart." We cannot give lip service to forgiveness; it must be totally genuine, without reservation.

- The only commentary Jesus offered about his Model Prayer was the phrase about forgiveness: "And forgive us our debts, as we forgive our debtors." Following the prayer, Jesus told His followers: "For if ye forgive men their trespasses, your heavenly Father will also forgive you: But if ye forgive not men their trespasses, neither will your Father forgive your trespasses" (Matthew 6:12–15). We may be uncomfortable with the idea that our forgiveness is tied to our willingness to forgive. Yet, Scripture offers this same admonishment not once but several times.

    o "And when you stand praying, forgive, if you have anything against any: that your Father also which is in heaven may forgive you your trespasses. But if you do not forgive, neither will your Father which is in heaven forgive your trespasses" (Mark 11:25–26).

161

> o "Judge not, and you shall not be judged: condemn not, and you shall not be condemned: forgive, and you shall be forgiven" (Luke 6:37).

15. If you are wrong, admit it. Confess your faults not only to the Lord, but to the person(s) you have offended. Scripture links healing to confession (James 5:16). Refusing to admit wrongdoing and resisting asking forgiveness increases internal stress. The other persons become a source of stress because they remind us of our guilt. Since we dislike the discomfort stress produces, we tend to avoid those people who are parties to our conflict.

Scripture declares that denying our sin means we are calling God a liar (1 John 1:10). However, at the same time, Scripture promises that "if we confess our sin, he is faithful and just to forgive us our sin and cleanse us from all unrighteousness" (1 John 1:9). Just as confession and repentance are keys to reconciliation and forgiveness from God, we need to humble ourselves to seek forgiveness from people we have offended (Matthew 5:23–24).

16. Emphasize God's honor.

It's not about us. When dealing with conflict, people tend to focus on themselves and the trouble. They may forget that how believers behave reflects on the name and reputation of God. Remind everyone involved that God's honor is at stake. Ultimately, the most important outcome lies not in who wins or in who gets his/her way, but whether God is glorified. Keeping the Lord's image in the forefront of the discussion motivates everyone to speak more kindly and to open themselves up to God's solution.

> *Ultimately, the most important outcome lies not in who wins or in who gets his/her way, but whether God is glorified.*

17. Find common ground.

During marriage counseling, I rarely begin by discussing the couple's problems. Talking about disagreements does not build a basis for healing wounded relationships. Instead, we talk about what attracted them to one another to begin with. As they recall good times and positive experiences, they recover common ground of the past on which to resolve current conflicts.

Common ground may involve agreement about issues. Before focusing on points of divergence, help each person to discover areas of agreement. At the famous Jerusalem Conference, the two sides came to the common agreement that God had brought salvation to the Gentiles just as He had to the Jews. The conditions of acceptance were agreeable to both parties. Peace was made and God was glorified (Acts 15).

Working with a church that was divided 60/40 on nearly all issues, I spent several weeks teaching about the importance of glorifying God in all things, including decisions about the church's future. In a series of meetings, we placed people around tables by random selection to force various parties to work together who had not been on speaking terms before. Tasking each table with deciding on five priorities for the church's future, but requiring unanimity before reporting to other groups, we left them to find common ground among themselves. After three weeks, each group shared their results. They discovered that they agreed on similar directions for the church after all. Having the first unanimous vote in years on those priorities led to ensuing joy and growth. Stress levels disappeared as the people committed themselves to one another and to the glory of God.

18. Discuss issues and solutions honestly and respectfully.

Instead of imposing solutions on others, invite all parties to share their viewpoints. Sometimes, the basic problem relates to a misunderstanding of how each one perceives the situation. Encourage questions to address any confusion as to what speakers mean by various statements. Discourage attacks on personalities by keeping the attention focused on the issues.

During the discussion, ensure a fair hearing by everyone. Often people will go along with different ideas if they feel others are giving them a genuine opportunity to present their positions. As participants debate the problem and possible solutions, work to keep communication flowing. Once people stop talking honestly and freely, resolutions become nearly impossible.

19. Commit the situation and solutions to the Lord.

Sincerely seek God's direction, surrendering personal desires. The best resolution may be totally different than any of those proposed by participants. Search the Scriptures for principles that may apply to the current problem. While specifics of the situation may be difficult to identify from biblical accounts, the Bible contains spiritual principles applied to every human dilemma.

Seek agreement in which people do not identify who wins or loses but rather a decision that glorifies Christ and, consequently, benefits His children. Such a result allows everyone to feel positively about the outcome and commit themselves to the ensuing direction.

What Do We Do If Conflict Is Not Resolved?

Jesus was the most Spirit-filled person ever to live; yet He constantly encountered opposition. In some situations, He resolved the conflict. In other places, He was rejected. In all cases, He loved the people involved, even when He rebuked them for their sin.

Sometimes conflict is unavoidable. You cannot control other people; you can only choose to behave in a peaceful, Christlike manner. Paul advised, "As much as it lies within you, live peaceably with all men" (Romans 12:18).

Give It Time

Some personalities get over personal pain quickly; others take much longer. The deeper and more emotional the hurt, the more time is required for healing. The old saying, "Time heals all wounds" is not exactly correct, because time alone does not heal. Still, over a period of time, people become more open to healing and reconciliation. Give God time to work in your heart and in the lives of others involved in conflict. The Lord can heal and reconcile in an instant; however, people have to yield to His Spirit. Prayerfully and patiently wait for God's healing touch, opening your heart so, at least for your part, God can bring freedom.

Trust the Lord

When we swallow our pride and initiate actions to produce reconciliation, we expect action. We look for results immediately. If others do not respond quickly, we wonder if we have wasted our time; we are tempted to doubt God's willingness to work. Don't give up. Trust the Lord to fulfill His promises. He wants His children to live in harmony. Trust His willingness and His ability to work reconciliation in His timing.

Love in Spite of the Conflict

Do not fail in letting God's grace continue to work. Avoid letting bitterness build a foothold in your life. Instead, love the other person as Jesus has loved you. "A new commandment I give unto you, That ye love one another; as I have loved you, that ye also love one another" (John 13:34). Jesus did not wait to love us until we responded to His grace. "But God commends his love toward us, in that, while we were yet sinners, Christ died for us" (Romans 5:8).

What if the other person does not respond positively to your advances toward reconciliation? Jesus teaches us by precept and example to love people, even when they maintain hatred toward us: "But I say unto you, Love your enemies, bless them that curse you, do good to them that hate you, and pray for them which despitefully use you, and persecute you; That ye may be the children of your Father which is in heaven: for He makes his sun to rise on the evil and on the good, and sends rain on the just and on the unjust" (Matthew 5:44–45).

Some Conflicts Will Not Be Resolved. Accept It and Move On

We mentioned earlier the contention between Paul and Barnabus over John Mark and the second missionary journey. The disagreement could not be resolved. Both were godly men, but were not able to reconcile their different commitments. Since their positions were irreconcilable, they agreed to move forward separately. Paul took Silas, and Barnabus left with Mark. The positive end of the story resulted in Paul's realizing John Mark's worthiness and asking Timothy to bring Mark with him, "For he is profitable to me for the ministry" (2 Timothy 4:11).

What About Church Discipline?

Yes, Matthew 18 teaches that the church should become involved in adjudicating a matter when someone refuses to deal with wrongdoing after private and, then, mediated admonishment. However, the purpose remains reconciliation. A prime example lies in the situation in the church at Corinth. Paul rebuked the church for not disciplining a man who was having an immoral relationship. Between First Corinthians and Second Corinthians, the sense of Scripture shows that the church disciplined the person and put him out of the fellowship. The man repented and Paul instructed the church to receive him back into the fellowship: "Sufficient to such a man is this punishment, which was inflicted of many. So that contrariwise you ought rather to forgive him, and comfort him, lest perhaps such a one should be swallowed up with overmuch sorrow. Wherefore I beseech you that you would confirm your love toward him. For to this end also did I write, that I might know the proof of you, whether you be obedient in all things. To whom you forgive anything, I forgive also: for if I forgave anything, to whom I forgave it, for your sakes forgave I it in the person of Christ; Lest Satan should get an advantage of us: for we are not ignorant of his devices" (2 Corinthians 2:6–11).

CHAPTER NINE

Marriage and Family Issues

One of the first lines of defense against overwhelming stress is a godly home. Just as the home is the basic building block of society, even so the family is the central component of ministry. The missionary home is the secure place where family members nurture one another, the base from which they launch ministry efforts, and the haven to which they can resort at the end of stressful days. Sustaining strong marriages and healthy families should be a top priority. The dynamics of life on the mission field (domestically or internationally) make these goals more difficult to attain and, at the same time, more important to maintain. The starting place commences with developing strong marriages.

Strengthening Marital Relationships

Parents cannot provide healthy environments for their children until they solidify their connections with one another as husband and wife. Many marriage counselors refer to Ephesians 5 when describing the qualities of a successful marriage. The godly husband loves the wife and gives himself to her sacrificially. The spiritual spouse submits to her husband as unto the Lord, trusting God to guide him as the spiritual leader of the home. While these truths are vital, they are only one aspect of healthy relationships. Additional principles for strong marriages include the following:

Base your commitment to each other on your commitment to Christ.

"Except the LORD build the house, they labor in vain that build it: . . ." (Psalm 127:1) In marriage counseling, I don't try to find out what couples' problems are first. Instead, we focus on each person's relationship with Christ. If both draw closer to Jesus, they will naturally come closer to one another. A successful, happy marriage begins with a husband and wife who love Jesus and live with Him as Lord.

Pray for one another and encourage each other in your relationships with Jesus. Reading the Scripture and worshipping together strengthen your mutual bond with the Lord and with one another. The more you love Christ, the stronger your affection will be for each other. In addition, your expression of devotion to Jesus and care for one another will provide a strong model for your children.

Treat one another as you want to be treated (Matthew 7:12).

Jesus' admonition to do unto others as we would want them to do unto us should be employed in the home before it can occur elsewhere. The New Testament's "one anothering" passages, mentioned earlier in this work, apply not only to relationships within the church but have special application to husbands and wives. Marriages grow stronger as husbands and wives exercise commitments such as these to one another:

- **Encourage one another to love and good work (Hebrews 10:24).** Loving spouses find ways not only to encourage one another in general, but specifically to "love and good works." Helping each other to express love in practical ways blesses the other person and provides a solid basis for mutual satisfaction.
- **Comfort and edify one another (1 Thessalonians 5:11).** Everyone gets down at times. Whenever a husband or wife experiences sadness, the other spouse need not try immediately to fix the problem but simply offer comfort and encouragement. Genuine empathy is one way to comfort one another. The Bible advises us to laugh with those who laugh and weep with those who weep (Romans 12:15).
- **Speak well to one another.** One never builds a marriage up by putting the other person down. How we speak to one another can edify and encourage or cause deep pain. Couples must guard their

communication. Avoid speaking in anger. Don't lie to one another (Colossians 3:8–9). Instead, use words to honestly share feelings without attacking the other person. Having the intention of helping one another, we will choose words that help and not hurt.

- **By love serve one another (Galatians 5:13).** Wedding vows in marriages I conduct use the phrase "Do you promise to love, honor, trust, and serve one another in sickness and in health, in adversity and prosperity and to be true and faithful to one another as long as you both shall live?" True love finds ways to serve the one who is loved. Husbands, don't wait until you are asked to help with the dishes. Pick up a rag and start washing! Wives, similarly, can find ways to serve their husbands with more than just a meal.

- **Be kind and affectionate toward one another (Romans 12:10).** Kindness makes deposits in relational accounts that sustain families during times of tension and stress. Genuine affection not only expresses itself in hugs and kisses but in kind words and deeds. Mark Twain observed: "Kindness is a language which the deaf can hear and the blind can see."

- **Confess your faults and pray for one another (James 5:16).** Instead of hiding or excusing errors, confess mistakes to one another. When one spouse offers honest, contrite confession, the receiving spouse responds with acceptance and forgiveness. Both husband and wife will find praying for each other a powerful tool for building strong relationships.

- **Grudge not one against another (James 5:9).** One test of genuine forgiveness involves whether a past sin comes back up in future arguments. Godly love does not bear grudges (1 Corinthians 13:5).

> *Godly love does not bear grudges.*

- **Forbear and forgive one another (Colossians 3:13).** The idea of forbearance involves restraint. When injured, our natural inclination is to lash out in anger and retaliation. Many marital struggles begin with reaction to pain. Paul's advice is to restrain oneself and forgive the other person. If we remember how Christ has forgiven us, we can find motivation to forgive others.

Appreciate the differences in your personalities.

Opposites attract, so the old saying goes. Often men and women with very different personalities marry. Sometimes they become frustrated with one another, often because they do not understand how each completes the other. When we first married, my wife and I had numerous occasions where our differing personalities clashed. Once we learned how our personality types complemented one another, we began to appreciate how God put us together so each one's strengths made up for the other's weaknesses.

At a retreat for pastors and their families in a new work (mission field) state, I led couples through a mutual testing using the DISC profile. Having been equipped by the North American Mission Board's Next Level Leadership Network (plus my own educational background in counseling), my seminar tried to help husbands and wives understand their individual personalities, those of their spouses, and how their differing types complemented each other.

Afterward, a couple asked to join my wife and me for lunch. They shared how they had been on the verge of divorce for two years. They couldn't understand why they had so many communication and relationship conflicts. They shared that the seminar showed them how their personality types not only could conflict, but how they could help one another. The Holy Spirit used this new understanding to help them appreciate their differences. They left the retreat with a new commitment to one another and to the work in which they were engaged.

Maintain communication.

During tension and stress, one of the first victims is communication. Men, especially, tend not to be communicative on a good day, unless we are teaching or preaching. Small talk is not our strong point. Under pressure, we tend to clam up even more. "How's your day, honey?" the wife might ask. "Okay," comes the grunted response. Wives may understand that their husbands are under stress, but they perceive the lack of communication as if their spouses are shutting them out.

Whether stress originates within the marriage or emerges from other causes, committed couples cannot yield to the temptation to withdraw emotionally. If tension has resulted from a perceived offense, a misspoken word, or hurtful action, husbands and wives must talk through the issue to a resolution. Simply downplaying or discounting the pain does not help. Simply saying, "Never mind; it's nothing," solves nothing.

Maintaining honest and kind communication helps solve problems, encourages others, and deepens relationships.

Keep the flame of love alive.

Many mission fields include exotic, even romantic, locations. However, when focused on the tough task of ministry, couples can find themselves missing a vital element of their relationship. In many average families, husbands and wives can fall into familiar routines that take each other for granted. Both forget the thrill of courtship amidst the fatigue of daily duties.

Wise husbands will look for opportunities to rekindle romance. While serving in state missions, I travelled fifty thousand miles a year in my car and had to spend two hundred nights a year in hotels. When I finally arrived home on Friday night, the last thing I wanted to do was get back in the car and go out for yet another meal that was not home cooked. Realizing my wife had been taking care of the children all week and working her own job as a piano teacher, I discovered ways to enhance our relationship. In our case, we spent Friday night at home as a family. We called it "Friday Family Fun Night," interjecting a good home-cooked meal with fun activities the entire family enjoyed. Then, on Saturday night, my wife and I usually had a date night. Without having to invest a small fortune in fancy restaurants or expensive places, we found many ways to revisit our courtship. Each date was a reinvestment in our relationship. After forty-two years of marriage, we still make weekly date nights an important part of our lifestyle.

Wives also have responsibilities to make romance work in the midst of hectic schedules and child raising. Families with children can sometimes trade off nights of child care, giving each couple some time alone. Candlelight dinners at home may be just as romantic as an expensive night at a four-star restaurant.

Husbands and wives should take care of their appearances. Men should realize that work, especially outdoors or in a mission environment without air conditioning, means they need to bathe and shave before reaching for a hug and a kiss. Wives in some mission locations may have to be creative in finding cosmetics or hair-care products. Still, the pleasure of renewed romance is worth the efforts of both.

Enjoy intimacy.

Sex is much more than a physical act; it should express the deepest emotional intimacy a husband and wife can experience. In the crowded schedule and close quarters of missionary housing, intimate relationships are difficult at best. Among the demands of children, ministry, travel, administrative needs, and other aspects of their lives, missionary couples may become stressed by the lack of private time together.

Husbands and wives may express frustration from inadequate emotional connection and affirmation in their marital relationship. Couples should make a priority of maintaining a high level of personal intimacy, emotionally and physically. As Paul said: "Let the husband render unto the wife due benevolence: and likewise also the wife unto the husband. . . . Defraud you not one the other, except it be with consent for a time, that you may give yourselves to fasting and prayer; and come together again, that Satan tempt you not for your incontinency" (1 Corinthians 7:3–5).

Resolve conflict quickly and quietly.

Every couple experiences disagreements. Unfortunately, some disagreements degenerate into conflict. The chapter on conflict management shares many principles that can be used in resolving marital disharmony. Here, let us focus on two key issues for resolving marriage conflict.

First, resolve struggles quickly. "Don't let the sun go down on your wrath" (Ephesians 4:26). Delaying solutions often makes matters worse.

Second, handle disagreements quietly. Some people grow up in homes where parents raised their voices when they argued. Others had homes characterized by peace and parents who worked out their problems without shouting. People often repeat the models of their childhood, bringing unhealthy patterns of coping into their marriages. Loud arguments rarely end well. "A soft answer turns aside wrath" (Proverbs 15:1).

Children often become fearful when they see or hear their parents' argue. When conflict continues or degenerates into shouting matches, children can be traumatized. They may begin having night terrors if they sense their security is threatened. On the other hand, some children may act out anger toward other children, siblings, or even the parents. Quick and quiet conflict resolution models a healthy approach for children and helps build stronger marriages.

With unconditional love for each other and total commitment to their marriage, husbands and wives can find ways to improve their relationships. Missionary couples can access numerous Christian books and other resources to give them additional insights into keeping their marriages strong. Peer and agency counseling help couples with difficulties resolve their differences. Their greatest aid is the Holy Spirit who works within each of them to meld the two into one.

Raising Godly Children

"Lo, children are a heritage of the LORD: and the fruit of the womb is his reward" (Psalm 127:3). Couples blessed with children understand the duality of pleasure and challenge they can be. Raising third-culture children on the mission field is challenging but provides a wonderful opportunity for both parents and children. This small section cannot address all the issues of child raising on the mission field, but includes four areas that tend to be especially stressful: childbearing, education, discipline, and dealing with prodigals.

Childbearing on the Field

Bearing children is stressful enough in the best of circumstances. Being on the mission field when children come into the world provides additional complications, which, while manageable, add to the pressure.

Available medical help. Many mission locations have at least adequate medical assistance for birthing; some venues are fortunate to have experienced midwives. When missionaries serve in remote locations, often many hours from doctors or hospitals, they try to plan, as well as they can, to spend the last weeks of pregnancy closer to medical help. Some couples even return to their stateside homes so extended family members can be part of the birth. However, complications can occur anytime. Missionaries may have to rely on whatever help is available.

Support systems. Building a support network in anticipation of childbirth can reduce the stress. Existing children may need someone to care for them while the parents are busy with the birth. Without the advantage of having extended family nearby, mothers-to-be rely more heavily on friends and fellow missionaries. As the birth approaches, communication with relatives back home will encourage the parents-to-be and ease the worry of potential grandparents. Sometimes, the extended family, especially the woman's mother, may be able to travel to the field and stay with the couple for a while to help out with other children, housework, cooking, and general encouragement.

Neonatal care. When newborns need advanced medical assistance, established agencies often provide emergency transportation to proper facilities. Still, with the best of care, seeing children in physical difficulty distresses the entire family. Having as much medical care during prenatal development can provide some advance warning of pending problems, giving the family more time to prepare. In such cases, families may choose to move closer to quality medical facilities.

Providing Education

Coming from a nation that appreciates quality education in both private and public sectors, missionary parents may find educating children and teens to be a challenge. Many choices are available, but each has its own stresses. Many countries have widespread public education, but locations where missionaries serve often do not have educational institutions other than private, usually church-related, schools.

Many parents choose to homeschool their children, particularly those in elementary school, although increasingly more high-school students are successfully homeschooled. The advantages include control over curriculum, convenience, costs, schedule flexibility, and security. Disadvantages can be stressful. Children may have difficulty separating the roles of the parent tasked with teaching (usually the mother). When are you the mom and when are you the teacher? When a child does not do well in schoolwork or becomes unruly, who exercises discipline—the mother or the teacher? In addition, the teacher/parent never has a break from interaction with the children, often producing burnout level stress. One answer involves several families creating a homeschool cooperative, in which parents share in various responsibilities. While problems can be overcome, the entire family has to work with one another to produce a happy solution.

Boarding schools provide another educational solution, especially for students in junior or senior high school. Again, this approach has positive and negative features. On the plus side, students have quality teachers in a controlled environment. Their peers are teenagers from similar backgrounds and often include students from diplomatic or other expatriate families. An obvious negative issue is separation from parents and siblings. Another concern involves the expense of the school, travel to and from the family's location, and other costs. Each of these problems can be the source of additional stress on the family and the child. However, the family that chooses this option can find spiritual and other resources to help them cope successfully.

Discipline and Discipling

Correction not only is necessary, it is an act of love. If a child or teenager misbehaves in attitude or action, only a truly unloving parent would ignore or excuse the problem. To allow disobedience to go on undisciplined encourages the child to continue down a destructive path. Scripture reminds us that just as a parent lovingly disciplines children, even so the heavenly Father corrects those He loves (Hebrews 12:6–7).

Discipline in typical families falls to the father. In some families, particularly if Dad has to travel often, the mother must take on the responsibility of providing discipline when the kids misbehave. Regardless of which parent executes discipline, the manner in which children are corrected is important. Paul warned that discipline should not be so harsh that children lose heart and rebel. "And, fathers, provoke not your children to wrath: but bring them up in the nurture and admonition of the Lord" (Ephesians 6:4). Incorrectly applied discipline is stressful on parents and children alike.

Scripture offers numerous parables about disciplining disobedient children. Corporal punishment, administered properly, remains one means of correction. At the same time, some children respond very poorly to spanking, especially if the parent is angry when handing out the punishment. Other methods are often effective, such as invoking a "time out" in which the child is isolated for a period to reflect on wrongdoing.

Consistency is vital for effective discipline. Application of correction should not vary widely from child to child or occurrence to occurrence. At the same time, parents should recognize the unique differences between children. As the late football coach, Bear Bryant, once said, "Some players are motivated by a pat on the back and some by a kick in the rump. The key to coaching is knowing which is which."

No one suggests parents ought to kick their children anywhere. The point is that sometimes the best correction is verbal; at other times, children need corporal punishment. In all situations, parents need to talk with their children about what was done, why it was wrong, how the action has hurt others, and what needs to be done to correct the situation. In some cases, discipline involves cleaning up a mess, apologizing for angry words, or helping someone else.

Another key to discipline is unity between parents. Parents should support one another when they have to correct a child. When possible, Mom and Dad will want to talk about how to handle disobedience. Where conferences are not possible, the absent parent should trust the best judgment of the disciplining parent and not allow the child to play one against the other. If parents differ greatly on how to discipline, they may experience stress in their own relationship. In no case should they play out their disagreements in front of the child.

A final consideration involves correcting attitudes versus behavior. Certainly, improper conduct needs discipline. Of greater importance, however, are attitudes behind the actions. If parents merely respond in kind to disrespectful words, facial expressions, body language, or other evidence of rebellious attitudes, they merely lower themselves to the child's level. As someone said, someone has to be the grownup!

Move from mere discipline to discipling.

Ultimately, parents want to move from mere discipline to discipling. They will have much greater long term success by building into their children the desire to please God and follow His Word than just correcting misdeeds. God has called us to make disciples of all people. Disciple making begins with our own households. By setting the example, by teaching principles of life from God's Word, by pointing out benefits of good decisions and harmful effects of poor decisions, and other such tools of discipleship, we can build into our children the desire to follow the Lord and honor Him.

The Pain of Prodigals

Everyone who knew Bob and Sandy thought they were the ideal ministry couple. They loved the Lord, their ministry, and their children. Coming to Christ as young adults, they had experienced difficulties prior to salvation but seemed to have moved forward in their Christian lives. That's why their children's behavior seemed so strange. Although raised in church with godly, loving parents, they began to rebel as they hit high school. Over the years that followed, they experienced divorces, trouble holding jobs, and other problems. Throughout their prodigal years, their parents continued to love them, pray for them, and minister to them. Although their hearts ached for their kids, Bob and Sandy kept trusting God to bring them back to Him and to them.

Faithfully serving on the mission field does not mean children and teenagers will not follow the ways of the prodigal son. Just like the son who left home, demanding his father's inheritance while rejecting his father's values, some young people rebel against their parents and their God (Luke 15:11–32). Some prodigals have never been converted and follow the natural tendencies of lost adolescents. Others have not been discipled or brought to spiritual maturity, and may fall prey to bad influences from peers. Still, others succumb to the temptations of the world, the flesh, or the devil, having chosen carnal lifestyles.

Pain produces pain: Teens who allow bitterness into their hearts over moving from family and friends may throw off parental constraint to hit back at parents (or even at God). This last situation is one reason why some agencies do not engage first-time missionaries with teenage children.

Pain inflicted by prodigals affects everyone around them. They suffer from their own misdeeds. Many do not continue in sinful patterns because they enjoy whatever they are experiencing but do so out of anger, fear, or pain. People who have been hurt tend to hurt others and incur injury to themselves at the same time.

Parents also experience pain through prodigals' attitudes and actions. In his important work, *Parents in Pain: Overcoming the Hurt and Frustration of*

Problem Children. John White observed that many parents struggle in their marriages when their children rebel. He notes that prodigal children can make a marriage stronger or tear it apart. Couples may struggle with each other, particularly when the mother and father disagree on the nature of the problem or the way toward solution. Their individual pain over their child's difficulties can be misdirected toward one another.[1]

Siblings, too, can be affected by prodigals' problems. Some may feel confused over the conflict and tension in the family. Younger children who look up to their older brothers or sisters may be tempted to follow in their footprints. Because the prodigal child becomes the focus of parental attention, other siblings may feel they are not as important. Like the elder son in the prodigal parable, they may be jealous when parents do more for the wayward ones. They wonder, "We've been good. So, why do Mom and Dad seem to love Billy (or Suzy or Tom or Jane) more?"

Ruth Bell Graham (Mrs. Billy Graham) has shared her experiences with the pain of prodigals. From the struggles of her own children to her observations of other parents whose children wander, she wrote: "For some reason, they (prodigals) are usually thought of as teenage boys. But prodigals are not limited in gender. . . . They do have one thing in common: They have left home . . . and they are missed."[2]

Ministry to prodigals: wait prayerfully. One way to respond to prodigals is merely to wait faithfully, watchfully, and prayerfully for their return. Mrs. Graham shares something of the heartache she and Dr. Graham endured waiting for their prodigals to come home. Yet the result was worth the wait. Like the prodigal in the parable, wayward children may eventually come to their senses and make their way home. In most cases, their investments of love and nurture will not prove fruitless (Proverbs 22:6).

The parents' role in waiting is to pray and to trust God to work in their children's lives. God loves both parents and child and will not abandon a lamb just because he or she has gone astray. God's ear is not deafened to the cries of a heartsick mother or father who cries out to Him for their children. Richard Burr's book, *Praying Your Prodigal Home*, urges praying families to maintain faith in a loving heavenly Father who is just as concerned about the prodigal as they. Effective prayers are rooted in faith, which in turn is founded on the Word of God, not mere wishes or emotions.[3]

Burr also reminds praying parents to make sure their own hearts are right before the Lord.[4] One of the key aspects is forgiveness. If prodigals perceive only judgment and punishment await them, they may prefer the relative safety of the far country. James wrote that prayer that avails much is not only fervent, but comes from a righteous soul (James 5:16). Only when we bring our own sins under the blood and forgiveness of Christ can we pray effectively.

Ministry to prodigals: wait expectantly. Another aspect of waiting is expecting. The father of the prodigal must have been in the habit of looking down the road his son took when he left home. Perhaps, he gazed down that lane each day, wondering if that would be the day his son would come home. Do you suppose he became tired or discouraged when his son did not return after many days? Perhaps, but the father did not give up and neither should you. Have faith and wait patiently on the Lord.

Sometimes parents want to rescue their children. Their sins put them in difficult and even dangerous situations. The prodigal of the parable lost all his money and became so hungry he took on a job no Jewish boy could imagine—tending pigs. He was so down and out he would have eaten the stuff the pigs were eating. What might have happened if the father had kept sending him money? Would this young man ever have come to his senses if his sin was rewarded by Dad getting him out of trouble every time God brought loving discipline into his life?

God loves us enough to bring us to a point of brokenness. Only through repentance—a change of mind that results in a change of life—can sinners (us included) find their way back to God. Sometimes it takes brokenness for us to experience repentance. At the same time, parents may need to intervene if their prodigals experience genuine danger. They may have fallen so far they cannot help themselves. They may want desperately for the parents to come and get them.

I received a call from a minister who needed help finding an eighteen-year-old daughter of one of his parishioners. The girl had run away from home and made her way to a large city where I was serving. Thousands of young people lived on the streets, and in worse places, because they felt anything was better than the restrictions of their home life. How was I to find this girl? Discovering she had called home, I used the phone number from which she called to find the address where she was staying. Being an adult, only she could choose to go back home. I tried to show her how much her parents missed her and wanted her to return. Her curt reply was, "If they loved me so much, why didn't they come get me instead of sending you?"

Ministry to prodigals: persevere in spiritual warfare. Although often rejected, parents and families of prodigals must persevere in prayer if they wish to prevail in the spiritual battle for their children. Quin Sherrer and Ruthanne Garlock chronicle the lives of numerous prodigals who ultimately returned to Christ and to their families. A consistent aspect of their strategy is consistent, fervent prayer. They advise, ". . . We must carry the prayer burden until we see results." Their approach to *Praying Prodigals Home* recognizes the ultimate enemy is Satan who has stolen precious lives. Families must engage in powerful spiritual warfare through prayer to "take back what the Enemy has stolen."[5]

Ministry to prodigals: provide a welcoming home. Many prodigals hesitate to return home for fear they will be rejected by family left behind. The father in the parable greeted his son with a hug, a robe (covering his shame), and a ring (a sign of assurance he was not to be treated as a servant, but a son). When prodigals return, the entire family needs to open their arms to the returning wanderer. Siblings who feel wounded by the prodigal's actions may resent the welcome parents give the sinner. Jesus' story reminds the entire family of the importance to receive the prodigals as no longer prodigals; they are brothers and sisters, sons and daughters.

Some prodigals may never respond, no matter how much love and prayer is offered. A few prodigals may be lost in the far country and not find their way back. Many, however, will wake up one day and realize how much they left behind. They have a family that loves them and waits for them. They have a heavenly Father who is willing to forgive and restore them. One day, waiting fathers and mothers will look down the lane and see the glad sight of a prodigal making his, or her, way home.

CHAPTER TEN

Extreme Stress: Burnout and Post-Traumatic Stress Disorder

Super stress, it might be called. Burnout and post-traumatic stress disorder (PTSD) are stress on steroids. Burnout is not as common as one might think, but when someone reaches this degree of unmanaged stress, strong measures should be taken to survive and thrive. PTSD is more discussed than experienced. Many people go through traumatic experiences, whether in war or violent crime, without falling prey to PTSD's insidious effects. Still, both conditions are very real and can be very dangerous.

Missionaries and their families are not immune to either condition. The good news for them and others is both problems can be overcome. Just as severe medical problems can be conquered with the correct treatment, even so, believers can find healing from burnout and PTSD.

What follows is not medical or psychological advice but observations and spiritual principles that offer hope to sufferers of each disorder. Persons who believe they are experiencing either of these problems should also seek competent help from appropriate Christian counselors or physicians. These few pages cannot offer comprehensive analysis of either issue. They are intended to provide spiritual insights and, most of all, hope.

Surviving Burnout

When stress continues unabated and unmanaged, burnout inevitably follows. This tertiary level of stress has been termed *exhaustion*. Most missionaries who reach this stage have strong enough spiritual commitment to avoid these types of responses. Still, many sufferers merely trudge through each day, feeling helpless and hopeless. Without help and spiritual renewal, many workers who remain at the burnout stage long enough will leave the mission field, adding to the attrition of the already thin mission force.

Evidence of Burnout

Burnout may manifest itself in depression, inability to engage in normal activities and responsibilities, lack of care for oneself and others, and a desire to escape. Some sufferers spend inordinate time in bed, trying to escape into sleep with the aid of whatever sedatives are available. Others may simply walk away—either from their jobs, their families, or both. A few escape life itself through suicide.

Glen Martin, in his book *Beyond the Rat Race,* describes several warning signs of stress overload: emotional and mental fatigue evidenced in constant feelings of discouragement, inability to enjoy life, impatience, perfectionism, spiritual disinterest, problems with relationships, and inappropriate priorities.[1]

Causes of Burnout

One of the most common causes of burnout involves focusing on the task to the exclusion of spiritual development. Without spiritual renewal and adopting proper priorities, missionaries can keep giving without taking in until they have nothing left for themselves or others. One study observed that burnout among workaholics is inevitable, especially among workers whose self-esteem is based on their productivity.[2]

An obvious contributor to burnout is sin. When we are out of God's will, we open ourselves up to spiritual attack from without and within. Satan's minions accuse us and we wallow in guilt. More importantly, God's Spirit brings conviction into the hearts of His children to draw them to repentance. David, King of Israel, reached that point. His story in Psalm 32 described how he arrived at the point where his bones seemed so brittle as to break and his strength was dried up within him. He spent all day groaning in misery (Psalm 32:3–4).

Ultimately, we could revisit all the various causes of stress because burnout can trace its roots to each of them. Whenever we experience sufficiently high levels of unmanaged stress over long periods of time, we are susceptible to burnout.

Effects on the Family

When the husband experiences burnout, the entire family experiences the effects. Their stress increases as they worry about his stress. Wives not only have their normal responsibilities at home, they also have a sick husband on their hands. His may not be a physical ailment, or his burnout may have led to various illnesses. He needs care, nonetheless. If burnout affects his ability to carry out ministry responsibilities, the wife usually has to fill in the gap. Her day extends into the night as she carries on correspondence, phone calls, planning activities, organizing preachers and other workers to take over engagements, and much more. Unless the husband and the wife get help, she may experience her own burnout.

Children see Dad going through this unusual change and feel threatened. The father may normally play or otherwise interact with them; now he comes home and may go straight to bed. He may have been fun; now he mopes around the house often showing little or no emotion. As they watch their mom expend extra time and energy to help ministry gaps, children and teens may actually become angry at the Dad, not understanding the nature of his problem.

Family Burnout

Family members are also susceptible to burnout. Burnout can strike anyone. Wives have their own challenges from persistent, pervasive stress. One study of over three hundred women revealed a strong correlation between burnout and incessantly trying to live up to everyone's expectations. From their study, Sue Eenigenburg and Robynn Bliss observed that not only does the woman have expectations of herself that may be unrealistic, but she also perceives strong expectations from her spouse and family, the mission agency and churches, coworkers, and the people of the culture in which she lives.[3] Trying to live up to unrealistic expectations can produce an unhealthy attempt at perfectionism, which is unattainable in this life. Strong inner forces can drive sufferers beyond the brink of burnout.

In addition, women experience pain as they watch their husbands undergo distress. In some cases, spouses can become codependent along with their husbands. They can come to enjoy being needed, while being stressed themselves by the caring process.

Children undergo their own sources of stress. Sometimes the parents are too caught up in their responsibilities, and perhaps their own levels of burnout, causing them not to notice the pain their MKs are experiencing. Keeping vigil over children becomes the responsibility of the entire family. Watch for signs of unusual lethargy, the lack of normal emotions, not wanting to engage in play with friends, and growing ambivalence toward activities that formerly generated excitement. Major changes of habits regarding eating and sleeping may also be evidence of abnormal stress. Parents would be wise to consult physicians, since the child may need medical care, as each problem may be a symptom of physical ailments such as malaria, a constant companion on many mission fields.

Recovery from Burnout

The term *burnout* seems to leave little hope. The word bears the image of someone so totally empty as to be irretrievably lost. Don't believe it! God does not leave His pilgrims in the "slough of despond," as John Bunyan described what we might call spiritual depression. He is able to heal, renew, and revitalize His children. God can heal in an instant, or He may choose to initiate recovery involving a number of steps:

Recognition. One of the first steps to overcoming burnout is to acknowledge you are experiencing it. Ministers may sense shame for not living up to what may be unrealistic expectations. Realize that godly people have gone through similar feelings. Moses came to the point of frustration and fatigue that he asked God to let him die (Numbers 11:14–15). After a miraculous victory over the prophets of Baal, Elijah was persecuted by

Jezebel. In his flight, he prayed that God would take his life (1 Kings 19:1–18). In both cases, God intervened and restored both to effective ministry. Missionaries should not be embarrassed or feel any sense of failure if they reach this level of stress. Greater men and women than they have suffered similarly. Their stories should encourage us to honestly appraise our situation and humbly seek help the Great Physician provides.

Reconnecting. Brooks Faulkner recommends a comprehensive program of defeating burnout, including attacking the problem on personal, professional, physical, and other levels. Coping strategies include reestablishing proper priorities, allowing intervention from peers and professionals, and seeking divine help from the Lord.[4] Maintaining freedom from burnout can be more successful with a network of support, including family, friends, and professional advisors from the mission agency's Member Care system.[5]

Sufferers should not shy away from seeking legitimate medical help. This recommendation does not suggest finding some pill to alleviate the symptoms alone. Rather, recognize that the exhaustion level of stress affects the body. A thorough physical can reveal if underlying medical problems, illnesses, or even cancer may be at the root of the various manifestations being experienced.

Renewal. Recognizing the brokenness in one's life, the next step to restoration is personal spiritual renewal. Joe Brown urges sufferers to rebuild the broken altars of their lives. Like Elijah at Carmel, taking the fallen stones of past worship, we can lay them again in order to call on the Lord for His power.[6]

As with other problems, people experiencing burnout need healing only God can supply. Part of their problem includes their inability or unwillingness to appropriate the power of the Lord. They may harbor sin they are unwilling to resolve through repentance and forgiveness.

> *"Healing can only take place when imbedded sin comes to the surface to be cleansed away. . . . The penitent sinner finds immense release."*
>
> *Donald Demaray*

They likely have ceased regular communion with Christ through prayer and Scripture meditation. Donald Demaray observes, "Healing can only take place when imbedded sin comes to the surface to be cleansed away. . . . The penitent sinner finds immense release."[7]

Reach out to God. Sometimes, burnout victims may be under such extreme exhaustion they are unable to do anything more than call out to God for help. He loves us and understands exactly where we are. He hears our cry and responds. The children of Israel cried to God in their distress and He responded with a deliverer—Moses (Exodus 2:23). When Israel came under persecution during the days of judges, they cried out to God and He sent a deliverer—Othniel, Caleb's younger brother, one of a series of judges who delivered the people of God from oppression (Judges 3:9).

Do you feel weak and helpless? God spoke of such people in terms of widows and orphans when He promised: "If thou afflict them in any wise, and they cry at all unto me, I will surely hear their cry" (Exodus 22:23). A Canaanite woman cried out to Jesus on behalf of her demonized daughter, and the ultimate Deliverer responded (Matthew 15:22ff). Even so, cry out to the Lord. He hears and responds with deliverance and healing.

Coping with Post-Traumatic Stress Disorder

Being in a different culture, often distant from law-enforcement protection or in a country hostile to Christians, missionary families face dangers on a regular basis. Increasingly, Westerners and Christians in general have become targets of terrorist attacks in public places. Some radical elements of hostile religionists instigate mass violence against the homes of believers or their churches. In addition, as in any location, they may fall victim to violent crime, home invasions, carjacking, kidnapping, and worse.

PTSD Reactions. People who experience severe trauma not only experience immediate stress reactions, but often have flashbacks, fear, anxiety, or other symptoms much later after the crisis has passed. The Mayo Clinic identifies PTSD symptoms. Some victims experience flashbacks or nightmares in which the trauma is relived. Others may express unwillingness to talk about the trauma even to the point of avoiding friends who want to help. They may be easily startled or seem jumpy. They may present a sense of helplessness and hopelessness. They may have trouble sleeping, feel restless, and express unexpected bursts of anger. Normal emotions may seem blunted as the sufferer falls into a depressive lethargy. They may begin using various medications (usually prescription drugs).[8]

Children and PTSD. Children often take more time to work through trauma than do adults. Charlesworth and Nathan observe: "They will withdraw, or, conversely, chatter about everything except the event until they feel safe enough to talk about the trauma. They may take even longer if there is no one whom they trust to reach out to them with sensitivity and patience to get them to talk about the event or act it out in play or artwork."[9] The National Institute of Mental Health (NIMH) warns that children who may suffer from PTSD may relapse into bed-wetting. They may constantly physically and emotionally cling to one or both parents and panic when separated.[10]

Responding to PTSD. One agency puts a team of counselors and helpers in place within twenty-four hours of such experiences. Care units not only provide counseling and help for the missionaries involved in the violence, but they also identify others affected by the trauma. On-the-field care is administered immediately with ongoing support until the personnel feel confident in continuing their work. If necessary, affected missionary families are brought home and given appropriate medical or other attention.

Secular organizations such as the National Institute of Mental Health and the Veterans Administration focus on various methods of counseling and psychotherapy, medications, and other treatments for PTSD sufferers. Certainly, victims should seek competent counsel, but believers will want to consult qualified Christian counselors who employ methods based on biblical principles. Whether certain medications are needed should be determined by the patients and physicians who take time to understand the spiritual, mental, and emotional aspects of the problem. Use of tranquilizers or antidepressants has come under increased scrutiny by such agencies as the NIMH. This writing is not intended to discourage proper medication but rather encourages believers to seek counselors and doctors who share common values.

Family and friends can also help PTSD victims, often simply by being around. Don't demand that the persons talk, but be available if they want to discuss their feelings. Victims can open up to someone who has recovered from a similar trauma. The more the sufferers can begin to verbalize their fears and talk about their experience, the sooner they can overcome its effects. Charlesworth observes that simply being held (physically) by family and close friends helps sufferers feel safer and reassured that they are safe. He also notes the need for victims to understand their reactions are normal in light of what they have experienced and they are not "out of control or going crazy."[11]

Families affected by crisis or trauma find mutual support for one another through prayer and practical means. The ministry of presence, just being there for one another, provides vital encouragement. Affected families often need help with basic needs, including food preparation, help with the children, and assistance with ministry responsibilities. Often, family members of colleagues have opportunities to lend aid as teens minister to teens and children share toys and play time.

Parents naturally give prime attention to supporting their children during crises. At the same time, they have to manage their own emotions. While adults try to remain strong for their children's sake, they need the freedom to express strong feelings. Delaying venting of emotions can set them up for post-traumatic stress disorder later. Competent counselors and compassionate friends offer safe harbors where fears, hurts, and other reactions can be shared.

Through every trial, the missionary's best comfort is the triune God whom they serve. They have a heavenly Father Who cares about each pain and hears every prayer. Their Savior, Jesus, intercedes for them at the right hand of the Father with the understanding of One Who suffered for them. The blessed Holy Spirit is a divine Comforter who comes alongside to strengthen and console them. With God's help, families can endure and experience healing.

Conclusion:

Hope!

Stress is part of life. Believers cannot opt out of stress, but we can equip ourselves not only to cope, but to overcome. God gives His children wonderful spiritual resources to help handle whatever comes our way, including stressful situations.

Christ's Body, the church, provides a welcoming fellowship of brothers and sisters with diverse backgrounds, experiences, and abilities. Within the church, we support each other, pray for one another, and contribute to each other's well-being.

God's Word includes amazing principles for life. Following God's precepts results in harmony and direction with God's purpose for our lives. Scripture guides our marriages and families, enhances our relationships with people, and helps us know Him.

The Holy Spirit actually lives inside the believer's spirit, bearing witness that we are God's children. He glorifies Jesus, convicts us of sin, intercedes with us in prayer, empowers us with His spiritual gifts, and produces His fruit in our lives.

Jesus, God the Son, loved us and laid down His life for us. He conquered death that we might have eternal and abundant life. He stands today ever living to make intercession for us. He is coming again to receive us to Himself so that where He is we can also be.

God, the heavenly Father, before He ever created us or a world to live in, saw our need for a Savior and fashioned an eternal plan none of us could imagine. "For God so loved the world, that he gave his only begotten Son, that whosoever believes in Him should not perish, but have everlasting life" (John 3:16). He is holy, majestic, all powerful, all knowing, ever present—and He wants us to have a personal relationship with Him through faith in His Son. Amazing!

With a God like that, we can face life with confidence and hope. We can experience lives of joy and abundance. We can overcome stress and anything else life throws at us, "For I am persuaded, that neither death, nor life, nor angels, nor principalities, nor powers, nor things present, nor things to come, nor height, nor depth, nor any other creature, shall be able to separate us from the love of God, which is in Christ Jesus our Lord" (Romans 8:38–39).

Endnotes

Chapter One

1. None of the names used in this work reflect actual identities of missionaries.
2. Interview with Member Care Leader. Agency not named for confidentiality.
3. Email from denominational missions director. Agency unnamed for confidentiality.
4. Hans Selye, *Stress Without Distress* (New York: Signet, 1975).

Chapter Two

1. Charles Solomon, *Handbook to Happiness* (Wheaton: Tyndale House, 1986), 38.
2. Robert S. Eliot M.D., *From Stress to Strength* (New York: Bantam Books, 1994), 45–46.
3. Miranda Ferrara, ed. *Human Diseases and Conditions*, vol. 4 (New York: Charles Scribers Sons, 2010), 1594.
4. American Medical Association, Charles Clayman, M.D., ed. *Family Medical Guide* (New York: Random House, 1994), 38.
5. Scott Litin, M.D., *The Mayo Clinic Family Health Book*, 4th ed. (Rochester, Minn: Mayo Clinic, 2009), 291–292.
6. Donald Demaray, *Watch Out for Burnout* (Grand Rapids: Baker, 1983), 14.
7. Litin, 293.
8. Eliot, 14.
9. Referenced in Kevin Leman, *The 6 Stress Points in a Woman's Life* (Grand Rapids: Fleming Revell, 1999), 34.
10. Taylor-Johnson Temperament Analysis (Thousand Oaks, California: Psychological Publications, Inc.).
11. Tim LaHaye, *Spirit-Controlled Temperament* (New York: Tyndale House, 1966).
12. Eliot, 4–5.
13. Edward Charlesworth, Ph.D. and Ronald Nathan, Ph.D. *Stress Management: A Comprehensive Guide to Wellness* (New York: Ballantine Books, 2004), 15.
14. Leman, 18–19.

Chapter Four

1. Litin, 292.
2. Martin Lloyd-Jones, *Spiritual Depression* (Grand Rapids: Eerdmans, 1965).
3. William Shakespeare, "Measure for Measure," Act 1, Scene 4.

Chapter Five

1. J. Herbert Kane, *Life and Work on the Mission Field* (Grand Rapids: Baker, 1982), 122.
2. Jerry Rankin, *Spiritual Warfare* (Nashville, B&H, 2009), 2–3.
3. Steven Lawson, *Faith Under Fire* (Wheaton: Crossway, 1995), xi.
4. Levi Keidel, *Conflict or Connection: Interpersonal Relationships in Cross-cultural Settings* (Carol Stream, Ill.: Evangelical Missions Information Service, 1996), 75ff.
5. American Medical Association, 27.
6. William Shakespeare, "Julius Caesar," Act 2, Scene 2.
7. Eliot, 5.
8. Roni Cohen-Sandler, *Stressed Out Girls: Helping Them Thrive in the Age of Pressure* (New York: Penguin, 2005), 8–10.
9. Litin, 221.
10. Pam Echerd and Alice Arathoon, ed. *Understanding and Nurturing the Missionary Family* (Pasadena, Cal.: William Carey Library, 1989), 174.
11. Reaching Beyond Borders "World Missions Facts," http://www.reachingbeyondborders.org/statistics.html
12. Kane, 85.
13. Ibid.
14. Interview with Member Care Leader, name and agency withheld for security reasons.
15. Terry Willis, *Parents as Partners: Supporting Your Family As They Serve Overseas* (Richmond: International Mission Board of the SDC, n.d.), 50.
16. Neal Priolo, *The Reentry Team: Caring for Your Returning Missionaries* (San Diego: Emmaus Road Intl., 2000), 36–39.

Chapter Six

1. Solomon, 50ff.
2. Bill Bright, "Have you made the wonderful discovery of the Spirit-filled

life?" Campus Crusade for Christ.

3. Hannah Whitehall Smith, *The Christian's Secret of a Happy Life* (New York: Fleming Revell, 1952), 46–47.

4. Ibid., 37.

5. Kane 126–7.

6. Echerd, 186.

7. Andrew Murray, *A Life of Obedience* (Minneapolis: Bethany House, 2004), 71.

8. John Piper, in address to the international staff of Campus Outreach, July 19, 2013.

9. Steven Lawson, *Faith Under Fire* (Wheaton: Crossway, 1995).

10. Larry Crabb, *Effective Biblical Counseling* (Grand Rapids: Zondervan, 1977), 164.

11. Johnson Oatman, Jr., "Count Your Many Blessings," 1897, public domain.

12. Solomon, 44–45. (For a good study of this subject, see Charles Solomon, *The Rejection Syndrome*. Wheaton: Tyndale House, 1988.)

13. Jay Adams, *Competent to Counsel* (Grand Rapids: Zondervan, 1970), 143.

14. Ferrara, 1598.

15. Adams, 93.

16. Richard Swenson, *Margin: Restoring Emotional, Physical, Financial, and Time Reserves to Overloaded Lives* (Colorado Springs: NavPress, 2004).

17. Martha Davis, Elizabeth Eshelman, and Matthew McKay, *The Relaxation and Stress Reduction Workbook* (New York: MUF Books, 1995), 35.

18. Suzannah Oliver, *Stress Protection Plan* (London: Collins and Brown, 2000), 59.

19. Willis, 9.

20. Interview with Member Care Leader.

21. Interview with National Missions Leader. Name and agency withheld for security reasons.

Chapter Seven
1. Myron Rush, *Management: A Biblical Approach* (Victor Books: 1983).

2. Ibid.

Chapter Eight

1. Charles Culpepper, *The Shantung Revival* (Crescendo Publications, 1976).

Chapter Nine

1. John White, *Parents in Pain: Overcoming the Hurt and Frustration of Problem Children* (Downer's Grove: InterVarsity Press, 1979), 104.
2. Ruth Bell Graham, *Prodigals and Those Who Love Them* (Grand Rapids: Baker, 1999), 11.
3. Richard Burr, *Praying Your Prodigal Home* (Camp Hill, Penn.: Wing Spread Publishers, 2003), 80ff.
4. Ibid.
5. Quin Sherrer and Ruthanne Garlock, *Praying Prodigals Home* (Ventra, California: Regal, 2000).

Chapter Ten

1. Glen Martin, *Beyond the Rat Race* (Nashville: B&H, 1995), 13–21.
2. Echerd, 172.
3. Sue Eenigenburg and Robynn Bliss, *Expectations and Burnout: Women Surviving the Great Commission* (Pasadena, William Carey Library, 2010).
4. Brooks Faukner, *Burnout in Ministry* (Nashville: Broadman Press, 1981), 118 ff.
5. Faulkner, 23ff, 133 ff.
6. Joe Brown, *Battle Fatigue* (Nashville: B&H Publishers, 1995), 187ff.
7. Donald Demaray, *Watch Out for Burnout* (Grand Rapids: Baker, 1983), 26.
8. Mayo Clinic, "Post-traumatic Stress Disorder," http://www.mayoclinic.com/health/post-traumatic-stress-disorder/DS00246/DSECTION=symptoms
9. Charlesworth, 123.
10. National Institute of Mental Health, "Post-traumatic Stress Disorder," http://www.nimh.nih.gov/health/topics/post-traumatic-stress-disorder-ptsd/index.shtml
11. Charlesworth, 125.

Bibliography

Abramowitz, Jonathan. *The Stressless Workbook*. New York: Guilford Press, 2012.

Adams, Jay. *Competent to Counsel*. Philipsburg, N.J.: Presbyterian and Reformed Publishing Co, 1970.

American Medical Association, Charles Clayman, M.D., ed. *Family Medical Guide*. New York: Random House, 1994.

Bright, Bill. "Have you made the wonderful discovery of the Spirit-filled life?" booklet, Campus Crusade for Christ.

Brown, Joe. *Battle Fatigue*. Nashville: B&H Publishers, 1995.

Burr, Richard. *Praying Your Prodigal Home*. Camp Hill, Penn: Wing Spread Publishers, 2003.

Charlesworth, Edward, Ph.D. and Ronald Nathan, Ph.D. *Stress Management: A Comprehensive Guide to Wellness*. New York: Ballantine Books, 2004.

Cohen-Sandler, Roni. *Stressed Out Girls: Helping Them Thrive in the Age of Pressure*. New York: Penguin, 2005.

Crabb, Larry. *Effective Biblical Counseling*. Grand Rapids: Zondervan, 1977.

Culpepper, Charles *The Shantung Revival*. Crescendo Publications, 1976.

Danielson, Edward. *Missionary Kid—MK*. Pasadena: William Carey Library, 1984.

Davis, Martha, Elizabeth Eshelman, and Matthew McKay. *The Relaxation and Stress Reduction Workbook*. New York: MUF Books, 1995.

Demaray, Donald. *Watch Out for Burnout*. Grand Rapids: Baker, 1983.

Echerd, Pam and Alice Arathoon, ed. *Understanding and Nurturing the Missionary Family*. Pasadena, Cal.: William Carey Library, 1989.

Eenigenburg Sue and Robynn Bliss, *Expectations and Burnout: Women Surviving the Great Commission*. Pasadena, William Carey Library, 2010.

Eliot, Robert S., M.D. *From Stress to Strength*. New York: Bantam Books, 1994.

England, Diane. *The Post-Traumatic Stress Disorder Relationship*. Avon, Mass.: Adams, 2009.

Ferrara, Miranda, ed. *Human Diseases and Conditions*, vol. 4. New York: Charles Scribers Sons, 2010.

Foyle, Marjory. *Overcoming Missionary Stress*. Wheaton: Evangelical Missions Information Service, 1987.

Graham, Ruth Bell. *Prodigals and Those Who Love Them*. Grand Rapids: Baker, 1999.

Harley, C. David. *Preparing to Serve: Training for Cross-cultural Mission*. Pasadena: William Carey Library, 1995.

Lawson, Steven. *Faith Under Fire*. Wheaton: Crossway, 1995.

Lloyd-Jones, Martin. *Spiritual Depression*. Grand Rapids: Eerdmans, 1965.

Jordan, Peter. *Re-entry: Making the Transition from Missions to Life at Home*. Seattle: Youth With A Mission, 1992.

Kane, J. Herbert. *Life and Work on the Mission Field*. Grand Rapids: Baker, 1982.

Keidel, Levi. *Conflict or Connection: Interpersonal Relationships in Cross-cultural Settings.* Carol Stream, Ill.: Evangelical Missions Information Service, 1996.

LaHaye, Tim. *Spirit-Controlled Temperament.* New York: Tyndale House, 1966.

Lawson, Steven. *Faith Under Fire.* Wheaton: Crossway, 1995.

Litin, Scott, M.D. *The Mayo Clinic Family Health Book*, 4th ed. Rochester, Minn: Mayo Clinic, 2009.

Leman, Kevin. *The 6 Stress Points in a Woman's Life.* Grand Rapids: Fleming Revell, 1999.

Margolia, Simeon, M. D. *The John Hopkins Medical Guide to Health After 50.* New York: Rebus, 2002.

Martin, Glen *Beyond the Rat Race.* Nashville: B&H, 1995.

Murray, Andrew. *A Life of Obedience.* Minneapolis: Bethany House, 2004.

Oliver, Suzannah. *Stress Protection Plan.* London: Collins and Brown, 2000.

Priolo, Neal. *The Reentry Team: Caring for Your Returning Missionaries.* San Diego: Emmaus Road Intl., 2000.

Rankin, Jerry. *Spiritual Warfare.* Nashville, B&H, 2009.

Rush, Myron, *Management: A Biblical Approach.* Victor Books: 1983.

Selye, Hans. *Stress Without Distress.* New York: Lippincott Williams & Wilkins, 1974.

Sherrer, Quin and Ruthanne Garlock, *Praying Prodigals Home.* Ventra, California: Regal, 2000.

Smith, Hannah Whitehall. *The Christian's Secret of a Happy Life*. New York: Fleming Revell, 1952.

Solomon, Charles. *Handbook to Happiness*. Wheaton: Tyndale House, 1986.

Swenson, Richard. *Margin: Restoring Emotional, Physical, Financial, and Time Reserves to Overloaded Lives*. Colorado Springs: NavPress, 2004.

Viser, William. *It's Ok To Be an MK*. Nashville: Broadman, 1986.

Willis, Terry. *Parents as Partners: Supporting Your Family As They Serve Overseas*. Richmond: International Mission Board of the SBC, n.d.

White, John. *Parents in Pain: Overcoming the Hurt and Frustration of Problem Children*. Downer's Grove: InterVarsity Press, 1979.

www.ingramcontent.com/pod-product-compliance
Lightning Source LLC
Chambersburg PA
CBHW031840090426
42741CB00005B/303